CROMWELL
VS
JAGDPANZER IV

Normandy 1944

DAVID R. HIGGINS

OSPREY PUBLISHING
Bloomsbury Publishing Plc
PO Box 883, Oxford, OX1 9PL, UK
1385 Broadway, 5th Floor, New York, NY 10018, USA
E-mail: info@ospreypublishing.com
www.ospreypublishing.com

OSPREY is a trademark of Osprey Publishing Ltd

First published in Great Britain in 2018

A catalogue record for this book is available from the British Library.

ISBN: PB 9781472825865; eBook 9781472825858;
ePDF 9781472825841; XML 9781472825872

18 19 20 21 22   10 9 8 7 6 5 4 3 2 1

Maps by bounford.com
Index by Rob Munro
Typeset by PDQ Digital Media Solutions, Bungay, UK
Printed in China through World Print Ltd.

Osprey Publishing supports the Woodland Trust, the UK's leading woodland
conservation charity. Between 2014 and 2018 our donations are being spent
on their Centenary Woods project in the UK.

To find out more about our authors and books visit
www.ospreypublishing.com. Here you will find extracts, author interviews,
details of forthcoming events and the option to sign up for our newsletter.

Acknowledgements
I would like to thank the following individuals for their kind support, without
which this book and my other military history endeavours might not have
been possible. Joseph Miranda, editor-in-chief, *Strategy & Tactics* magazine;
Colonel (ret.) Jerry D. Morelock PhD, editor-in-chief, *Armchair General*
magazine; Christian Ankerstjerne; and my editor, Nick Reynolds. Any errors
or omissions in this work were certainly unintended, and I alone bear
responsibility for them.

Author's note
In this book, German-language designations have been retained for German
ranks, units and formations, while Allied combatants are designated in
English. Metric measurements are used throughout the book. Unless otherwise
noted, all references to the Jagdpanzer IV refer to the L/48 variant.

Glossary

APCBC-HE	Armour-Piercing Capped Ballistic Cap – High Explosive
APCBC-T	Armour-Piercing Capped Ballistic Cap – Tracer
APCR	Armour-Piercing Composite Rigid
APDS	Armour-Piercing Discarding Sabot
HE	High Explosive
HEAT	High Explosive Anti-Tank

Imperial War Museums Collections
Many of the photos in this book come from the huge collections of IWM
(Imperial War Museums) which cover all aspects of conflict involving Britain
and the Commonwealth since the start of the twentieth century. These rich
resources are available online to search, browse and buy at www.iwm.org.uk/
collections. In addition to Collections Online, you can visit the Visitor Rooms
where you can explore over 8 million photographs, thousands of hours of
moving images, the largest sound archive of its kind in the world, thousands of
diaries and letters written by people in wartime, and a huge reference library.
To make an appointment, call (020) 7416 5320, or e-mail mail@iwm.org.uk
Imperial War Museums www.iwm.org.uk

Title-page photo: A Cromwell IV advancing south of Caen in early August
1944. (Conseil Régional de Basse-Normandie/Archives Nationales du
CANADA/Wikimedia/Public Domain)

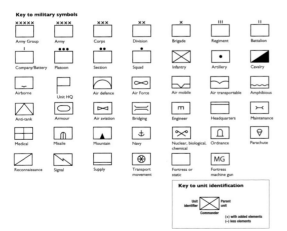

Key to military symbols

CONTENTS

INTRODUCTION

With German resources stretched and the Axis on the strategic defensive, repurposing existing offensive tank chassis into turretless tank-hunters, such as the Jagdpanzer IV, allowed the vehicles to have a comparatively smaller profile, and heavier armour and firepower, albeit with considerably reduced elevation and traverse. This Jagdpanzer IV from Panzerjäger-Abteilung 228 (116. Panzer-Division), displaying some side-skirt armour, is missing its muzzle brake. Following D-Day, 116. Panzer-Division spent several weeks to the north-east of the Normandy battle zone in anticipation of an invasion at Pas-de-Calais. Relocated to the Saint-Lô area in late July 1944 to help stem the American break-out, the division would be nearly destroyed during the Falaise–Chambois Pocket fighting on 20/21 August. (Bundesarchiv Bild 101I-585-2194-34A Foto: Appe (Arppe))

At just after midnight on 6 June 1944 the Allied nations, including the United Kingdom, United States, Canada and Poland, began their long-anticipated amphibious invasion of north-western Europe via the Normandy region of German-controlled France. Following an Allied naval and aerial bombardment and the deposit of US and British airborne forces on the flanks of five main landing zones spread along 80km of coastline, at 0630hrs First (US) Army forces began landing in the west, on Utah and Omaha beaches. An hour later, elements of Second (British) Army initiated landings on Gold, Juno and Sword beaches in the east, where they sought to capture the key communications hub of Caen as a precursor to advancing into the open terrain beyond.

At Gold Beach the reinforced 50th (Northumbrian) Infantry Division pushed ashore along its 8km section of coast against greater resistance than anticipated from

4

Organized along British lines, Poland's 1st Armoured Division operated tanks such as the Cromwell IV shown here, with its crew and a cameraman, in the months before the division entered combat in August 1944. Having been relocated from Scotland south to Scarborough, North Yorkshire, in preparation for commitment to the Normandy front, 10th Mounted Rifle Regiment, the division's reconnaissance regiment, continued to train. In combat this unit's Cromwells would be tasked with determining enemy locations, movement and activity times and the identification of enemy formations, often at considerable distance from other elements of the parent division. An armoured reconnaissance regiment in British service was expected to deny similar intelligence to the enemy, while providing accurate, timely communication with higher headquarters. Although the Cromwell's engine was considered rather noisy for scouting duties, constant improvements in German weapons and manoeuvrability meant the Cromwell represented a considerable improvement over armoured cars and light tanks such as the Stuart III/V, as in addition to statically watching enemy activity, heavier tanks could draw fire, engage targets and conduct operations more aggressively. Individual reconnaissance assets were expressly dissuaded from operating in dual roles that drew them into static positions and degraded their freedom of manoeuvre, although sub-units could be so divided and allocated as needed when circumstances warranted. (National Digital Archive, Poland/CCO 1.0)

716. Infanterie-Division and assorted security and combat units. With 8th Armoured Brigade in support, 56th (Independent), 69th and 151st Infantry brigades fanned out to capture Arromanches and make contact with the Americans and Canadians, at Omaha and Juno beaches respectively, by day's end. With Second (British) Army's generally cautious advance, poor weather and an active, but largely piecemeal, German response from 21. Panzer-Division and the adjacent 12. SS-Panzer-Division *Hitlerjugend* prevented the Allies from capturing Caen. Although SS-Panzerjäger-Abteilung 12 had arrived west of Paris at Nogent-le-Roi on 24 May 1944 it spent the next two months conducting training, maintenance and limited repositioning closer to the Normandy front.

With the British having employed a predominantly infantry force to secure a beachhead, on D+1 Maj-Gen George W.E.J. Erskine's 7th Armoured Division landed and soon helped secure the Bayeux area. As its 22nd Armoured Brigade's 1st Royal Tank Regiment (1st RTR), 5th RTR and 4th County of London Yeomanry (4th CLY) employed Britain's new Cromwell tank, Erskine's command seemed well-suited for pushing through the constricted *bocage* (hedgerow) country around Tilly-sur-Seulles and Villers-Bocage and into the open terrain to the south-east before German reinforcements arrived in strength. To counter this bid to outflank Caen from the west, some 60km to the south Generalleutnant Fritz Bayerlein's Panzer-Lehr-Division was rushing to the scene in anticipation of helping throw Second (British) Army back into the English Channel. As part of this formation the crews of Panzerjäger-Lehr-Abteilung 130's new turretless Jagdpanzer IV tank destroyers intended to apply their mounts' powerful main armament and low profile to ambush enemy armour from obscured, largely stationary positions.

CHRONOLOGY

1921
27 October   Poland's 10th Mounted Rifle Regiment is established.

1939
3 September   4th County of London Yeomanry (Sharpshooters) is created.

1940
24 June   The first British 'Tank Board' committee is created.

1941
17 January   A second 'Tank Board' proposes developing Nuffield's A24 Cavalier (Cromwell I).

April   PzKpfw IV Ausf F production begins.

20 June   The 'Tank Board' orders 1,000 Cavalier tanks to be produced.

1942
January   Cavalier prototype is completed.

20 January   Factory testing of the A27M (Cromwell) commences.

March   7.5cm PaK 39 L/48 is introduced into German service.

29 April   Two A27L Centaur (Cromwell II) prototypes are ordered to be built.

29 June   One A27L prototype is completed.

2 October   Hitler is shown plans for a new *Jagdpanzer* mounting a 7.5cm KwK 42 L/70 cannon.

1943
3 January   Vickers is instructed to produce the 75mm Royal Ordnance Quick Fire Mk V cannon.

February   Cromwell I production begins.

A Royal Electrical and Mechanical Engineers (REME) sergeant welding damaged armour on a Cromwell IV on 8 August 1944 at a 29th Armoured Brigade workshop. The vehicle is from 4 Troop, C Squadron, 2nd Northamptonshire Yeomanry. Its 11th Armoured Division yellow, red and black bull emblem is to the right of the bow machine gun. (© IWM B 9098)

A knocked-out Cromwell IV, which was produced by the Birmingham Railway Carriage & Wagon Co., Ltd. In addition to the Germans removing anything of value, as evidenced by the open trackguard stowage lockers, both vehicles sport a field modification of a metal mesh stowage basket affixed to the turret rear; possibly made from exhaust cover meshes. The right-hand Cromwell also has a welded framework at its rear for carrying additional equipment. When idling or moving at slow speeds Cromwell drivers needed to maintain high RPMs to avoid sparkplug fouling, although this reciprocally increased engine noise. Road-wheel axles were prone to bending in rugged terrain and vehicle tow hooks were found to be weak for most use. (PHAS/UIG via Getty Images)

14 May	Vomag exhibits a wooden mock-up of the proposed Jagdpanzer IV to Hitler.
October	The Cromwell IV is first distributed to British armoured formations.
20 October	Vomag completes a soft-steel Jagdpanzer IV prototype.
20 December	0-Series Jagdpanzer IV prototype is shown to Hitler.

1944

January	Jagdpanzer IV (L/48) production begins.
10 January	Panzerjäger-Lehr-Abteilung 130 is established as part of the Panzer-Lehr-Division.
2 February	Production Cromwell model is finalized.
6 February	SS-Panzerjäger-Abteilung 1 is allocated to 12. SS-Panzer-Division *Hitlerjugend* as SS-Panzerjäger-Abteilung 12.
March	Jagdpanzer IV's port pistol opening is sealed.

17/18 March	Panzerjäger-Lehr-Abteilung 130 receives 31 Jagdpanzer IVs.
24 May	SS-Panzerjäger-Abteilung 12 receives ten Jagdpanzer IVs.
6 June	Operation *Overlord* (D-Day) begins.
7–14 June	Operation *Perch* begins as a British effort to bypass the seemingly open German left flank at Caen.
13 July	SS-Panzerjäger-Abteilung 12 receives 11 Jagdpanzer IVs.
8–13 August	Operation *Totalize* commences to push south of Caen and help close the 'Falaise Gap'.
November	Jagdpanzer IV (L/48) production ends, being replaced with designs incorporating a longer 70-calibre cannon being produced from August 1944.

1945

January	Cromwell production ends.

DESIGN AND DEVELOPMENT

CROMWELL

ORIGINS

Although the British developed and fielded the world's first tanks in 1916, which once applied in sufficient numbers and properly supported helped bring operational manoeuvre to a largely static Western Front during World War I (1914–18), throughout the 1920s the high economic cost of victory translated into drastic cuts in military spending, high unemployment and disarmament that undercut the development of armoured and mechanized forces. During this post-war period conservative, traditionalist senior commanders were resistant to raise armoured forces to the same standing as traditional artillery, infantry and cavalry, or incorporate tanks into the British Army's structure. Although some credibility was afforded to the fledgling battlefield asset with the creation of the Royal Tank Corps in 1923, the best way to design and use armoured fighting vehicles (AFVs) remained unclear into the 1930s. Unlike many officers who envisaged tanks as simply continuing their plodding infantry-support roles, others, such as J.F.C. Fuller and to a lesser degree Basil Liddell Hart, advocated their use in operational-level exploitation and pursuit actions – either as massed tank fleets operating independently, or within a mix of armour, artillery and motorized infantry.

To accommodate these differing perspectives, by 1936 the British Army had gravitated towards three main tank types: reconnaissance (light) tanks; exploitation and pursuit (cruiser) tanks, which the specialists favoured; and traditionalist-promoted

infantry-support (heavy) varieties. Effective implementation, however, remained a challenge due to the complex and bureaucratic organization behind tank design and production that stifled efficiency, unity of purpose and progress. While the War Office's Department of Tank Design was established in 1931 to issue specifications and suggest improvements to the final products, a situation which continued as Britain re-armed and other companies were brought into AFV production, tank designs remained the purview of the individual firms. In an effort to orchestrate subsequent tank design, development and production, in 1927 the War Office established a Directorate of Mechanisation to coordinate with tank manufacturers. In August 1939 the new Ministry of Supply was given control over supplying Britain's armed forces and took over responsibility for the provision of weapons to the Army; but in its effort to improve the volume of weapon production, including tanks, the department's collaboration with producers was often tenuous.

With both British Houses of Parliament expressing concern to Prime Minister Neville Chamberlain at the apparent monopoly the Director General of Tanks and Transport had over tank production, a 'Tank Board' committee was created (24 June–25 November 1940) to coordinate tank development and production. Under the direction of representatives from the Ministry of Supply, the War Office and the manufacturers, the organization served only to advise and report, although it gradually gained more authority over tank design and procurement. To coordinate General Staff requirements, and Ministry of Supply demands based on government munitions policies, industrial capacities and a fluctuating labour force, additional tank boards were subsequently formed. Although this period was fraught with contrasting priorities, 'scope creep' and inefficiencies, circumstances changed in September 1942 when an all-encompassing fifth 'Tank Board' was created, tasked with continually scrutinizing the qualitative aspects of tank design and production. To prevent separate companies from producing their own tank designs in isolation, 'groups' were formed, with one firm acting as a 'design parent'.

DEVELOPMENT

With the Directorate of Tanks and Transport calling for a tank to replace the ageing A15 Crusader, and mount the new QF 6-pdr cannon, the General Staff specified an A23 based on a smaller version of Vauxhall's A22 Churchill infantry tank, as well as

A Covenanter tank leads several Crusader tanks of Poland's 1st Armoured Division during training exercises in early 1944. In an effort to produce a lighter, faster alternative to the A16 cruiser design the British War Office contracted out the development of what was designated the Covenanter, Cruiser Mk V, A13 in 1937. The 18-tonne vehicle possessed sloped armour (welded hull, riveted turret), a 7.92mm Besa machine gun and a 2-pdr main gun, which by 1939 standards was increasingly inadequate for anti-tank roles. As a consequence of the looming European war, heavy-manufacturing resources generally lacking expertise in armoured vehicle design and a rushed production the Covenanter suffered from mechanical problems, especially with its awkwardly positioned radiator. Save for the Matilda II, and perhaps the Valentine, contemporary British tank designs were generally under-gunned and under-armoured, and struggled to maintain battlefield viability against their PzKpfw III and PzKpfw IV opponents. To address these issues, in July 1940 the War Office issued a specification for a new cruiser tank that featured thicker armour and a sufficiently large turret to mount the new QF 6-pdr cannon. Until these Cromwell and Comet designs became available, however, the A15 Crusader just entering mass production would serve as an interim solution. (© IWM MH 1135)

9

The Cromwell I was armed with an unmodified 6-pdr main gun, and was used only for training. Pictured in Scarborough during the summer of 1944, this driver and machine-gun operator from Poland's 10th Mounted Rifle Regiment ham it up for the camera. The front plate is inscribed with 'THIS VEHICLE IS FILLED WITH ANTI-FREEZE 1/3 2/3 & MUST NOT BE DRAINED'. The turret has '...TURRET...CHECK SCALED...INTACT'. Note the starboard mirror to assist the driver when reversing, and the horseshoe talisman in the 'down' position to bring good luck to the crew. (Czesław Datka/National Digital Archive, Poland/CCO 1.0)

an A24 for Nuffield Mechanizations Ltd's cruiser design. The Birmingham Railway Carriage and Wagon Company was similarly tasked. With Wolseley Aero Engines Ltd having purchased Nuffield Mechanizations Ltd in 1937, the latter had worked on a 24-tonne design since mid-1940 that included an improved 410bhp (306kW) Liberty engine producing a top speed of 40km/h. On 17 January 1941 a second 'Tank Board' chose Nuffield to commence vehicle production in early 1942. To save time and reduce costs, much of the A15 Crusader's components were to be used for the first six prototypes of the A24 Cavalier. As Nuffield struggled to maintain other projects and remain on schedule, in late 1941 Ruston & Hornsby Ltd was brought in to produce what was rechristened the Cromwell. Vehicle trials began in March 1942, during which time the Liberty engine, with its 14.1bhp/tonne (10.5kW/tonne), was deemed underpowered, and the Cavalier was soon relegated to training functions.

Having travelled to the United States in late 1942 the British Tank Engine Mission considered using the American 493bhp (368kW) Ford V8 engine as an alternative to the more powerful Meteor. While the Ford V8 was easier to produce, the 'Tank Board' refrained from instituting the change, in part because the Cromwell's rear layout, and the location of its cooling system and other components, made the engine change difficult.

With the conversion of the Rolls-Royce Merlin engine that powered the Spitfire fighter and Lancaster heavy bomber, and later the P-51 Mustang fighter, found to be suitable for use in AFVs, in early 1942 Rolls-Royce was tasked with providing its Meteor equivalent. Although powerful, the Meteor's cooling and manufacturing problems prompted Leyland Motors temporarily to install an improved NML Liberty engine to allow their A27L ('Liberty') Cromwell II (later designated the Centaur I) to enter production in November 1942. Although the Cromwell was the first production tank to incorporate the Meteor engine, the Ministry of Aircraft Production was initially reluctant to redirect their Merlin engine resources from aircraft development until the summer of 1942, and it was not until October that year that 2,000 tank engines were ordered. Because the Royal Navy had priority on diesel fuel, and the Royal Air Force on high-octane petrol, the Army was reliant on lower-octane pool petrol, which was less flammable, and more commonly available than diesel, although it was less fuel-efficient.

By early 1943 the British experience in North Africa translated into a prioritization of speed and mobility and a diminishing value being placed upon slower infantry tanks. With infantry tanks remaining in production to maintain quantity AFV output, however, the effort directed towards producing new designs correspondingly suffered. In late February 1943 a final 'Tank Board' decided that Vickers-Armstrong Ltd should

A Cromwell II prototype with wider tracks and no bow machine gun undergoing trials. Note the appliqué armour fitted to the hull front and turret. With British tank manufacturers finally moving away from riveting to welding, thicker Rolled Homogeneous Armour (RHA) plates were incorporated into hulls and turrets, with stronger seams and no need for bolt holes that reduced plate integrity. As the largely wasted British effort of manufacturing outdated designs to maintain production numbers was finally waning due to the influx of foreign vehicles, and the advent of the Cromwell, the quality and quantity of subsequent designs benefited. As evidence, the later Centurion would represent Britain's best wartime design, and although it was fielded too late for combat operations, it heralded a departure from the multi-vehicle solution and a move towards an all-encompassing main battle tank of the kind long envisaged by General (later Field Marshal) Bernard Montgomery, and others. (© IWM MH 9300)

move their tank-building capacity over to producing the Cromwell; if the design proved inadequate within six months, production would be cut and additional US-built tanks would be obtained. Presenting a more promising option, Birmingham Railway Carriage and Wagon Company had been working on a design using the Meteor engine. A shortage of these engines meant that Leyland Motors was tasked to provide a third variant of the new tank, the A27L Centaur, fitted with an upgraded Liberty engine. The Centaur's development ran parallel to that of the Cromwell, but reliability issues meant it continually struggled in service trials, and like the Cavalier, it was withheld from front-line service.

In early 1943 the General Staff decided that 7,600 infantry and cruiser tanks were to be produced during 1944, but by July 1943 Prime Minister Winston Churchill approved a reduction in the programme to 6,900 and the acceptance of an additional 3,000 US-built tanks. As late as September 1943, an important issue was raised: although the Cromwell was at least as good as the M4 Sherman, the British tank lacked the ability to be up-gunned beyond its 75mm cannon.

Ultimately, 503 Cavaliers and 1,821 Centaurs were constructed; given that they were withheld from combat, the effort unnecessarily detracted from producing more effective designs. The desire to avoid disrupting tank production resulting from major factory changeovers resulted in 1,650 Crusaders and 1,798 Valentines being built in 1943, compared to 532 Cromwells. In 1944 the Cromwell programme would finally receive priority, with other firms being brought in to increase production.

PRODUCTION

The Cromwell I was nearly identical to the Centaur I, save for the Cromwell's Meteor engine, with 357 eventually produced. A subsequent Cromwell II incorporated wider tracks and increased stowage, but lacked a machine gun. As a Vauxhall project the

11

A27M CROMWELL IV SPECIFICATIONS

General
Production run: October 1943–January 1945 (15 months)

Vehicles produced: 1,935

Combat weight: 28,000kg

Crew: five (commander, gunner, loader/radio operator, driver, co-driver/machine-gunner)

Dimensions
Length (hull / overall): 6.35m / 6.42m

Width: 2.91m

Height: 2.49m

Armament
Main gun: 75mm ROQF Mk V L/36.5 (64 rounds (23 turret / 41 hull))

Elevation: -12 degrees to +20 degrees

Sight: No. 50×3 L Mk I (or ML Mk II) (3×, 13 degrees)

Secondary: 2×7.92mm Besa machine gun (coaxial; bow) (4,950 rounds in 22 belts)

Turret rotation (360 degrees): 15 sec (hydraulic); 40 sec (manual)

Armour (degrees from vertical)
Glacis: 25mm @ 58 degrees

Hull front (upper / middle / lower): 64mm @ 0 degrees / 57mm @ 22 degrees / 25mm @ 62 degrees

Hull side (upper / lower): 14mm + 32mm @ 0 degrees / 14mm + 29mm @ 0 degrees

Hull rear (upper / middle / lower): 25mm @ 0 degrees / 32mm @ 10 degrees / 20mm @ 45 degrees

Drive housing (upper / lower): 32mm @ 16 degrees / 14mm @ 57 degrees

Hull roof: 19mm @ 90 degrees

Engine deck: 14mm @ 90 degrees

Hull bottom (front / rear): 8mm + 6.35mm @ 90 degrees / 6.35mm @ 90 degrees

Turret front: 64mm + 12.7mm @ 0 degrees

Turret side: 51mm + 12.7mm @ 0 degrees

Turret rear: 44mm + 12.7mm @ 0 degrees

Turret roof (forward / rear): 19mm @ 13 degrees / 19mm @ 90 degrees

Turret bottom: 19mm @ 90 degrees

Communications
Internal: Wireless Set No. 19 (IC Channel)

External: Wireless Set No. 19 included an A set with a 16km range for communicating with command, and a 910m-range B set to communicate between the formation's tanks.

Motive power
Engine: Rolls-Royce Meteor 4B (or 4B/1) 12-cylinder (water-cooled) 26.9l (petrol; designed for 67 octane)

Power to weight (sustained): 650bhp (485kW) @ 2,550rpm (23bhp (17.2kW)/tonne)

Transmission: Merritt-Brown Z.5; five forward, one reverse

Fuel capacity: 527l in three tanks

Performance
Ground pressure: 1.05kg/cm^2

Maximum speed (maximum / road / cross-country): 62km/h / 41km/h / 29km/h

Operational range (road / cross-country): 265km / 180km

Fuel consumption (road / cross-country): 0.50km/l / 0.34km/l

Fording: 1.22m

Step climbing: 0.91m

Climbing (ascending / descending): 25 degrees / 25 degrees

Trench crossing: 2.29m

Ground clearance: 0.41m

A27M CROMWELL IV, 10th MOUNTED RIFLE REGIMENT

In April 1944, as per Army Council Instructions (ACI) 533, Cromwells were to have their SCC No. 2 Brown coat overpainted in SCC No. 15 Olive Drab – as shown here – to match that of US-made vehicles, but with only a few weeks until D-Day some vehicles retained their old colour. A textbook application of Cromwell markings included the War Department (WD) number or census mark (T xxxxxx) in white, which was to be affixed on the lower front and rear plates, and both turret sides. To provide information about the tank's ability to cross bridges, it bore a yellow oval enclosing the vehicle's tonnage.

Polish Cromwells utilized the same basic marking system as the British, save for adding a black winged Hussar symbol within an orange circle heralding the formation's cavalry heritage dating back to the regiments of mounted rifles during the Napoleonic Wars. As a reconnaissance unit, 10th Mounted Rifle Regiment's Arm of Service marking was a white '45' within a half-green/half-blue square, with white tactical symbols. The regimental colours were green and yellow separated by a thin white insert, while squadron pennant squares indicated HQ Squadron (black), 1st (red), 2nd (white) and 3rd (yellow). A 'PL' within an oval on the rear-left, outboard of the unit flash, was added immediately before Operation *Totalize* to indicate 'Free Polish Forces'. White Allied stars, each within a surrounding 10cm-wide circle, were painted on the vehicle's hull sides or on its stowage bins, while some of Polish 1st Armoured Division's subordinate units painted over all markings except unit flashes for operational security.

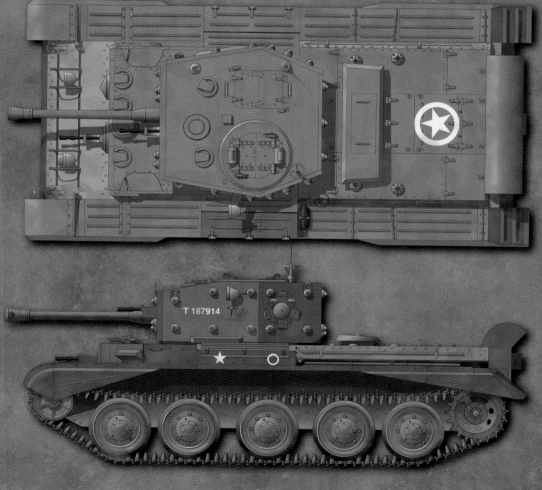

6.42m

prototype had a cast turret similar to that of the company's redesigned Churchill VII infantry tank, and was created in minimal numbers and never for production, as the company continued to produce the Churchill beyond its proposed 1943 cancellation. As a separate development track from the Cromwell I, the Centaur I resulted in the Centaur III and Centaur IV, Centaur AA Mk I and Cromwell III, which had been upgraded with an early Meteor V12 engine. Only 200 were so converted due to limited Centaur I numbers. The first three Cromwell designs mounted a 6-pdr (57mm) ROQF (Royal Ordnance Quick Fire) main gun minus a muzzle brake. The North African campaign (1940–43) highlighted the need for a more powerful armament that used the same 75mm ammunition as the M4 Sherman's M3 main gun. With the Centaur III equipped with the 75mm ROQF Mk V/VA L/36.5 cannon and upgraded with the Meteor engine, it began production in January 1944 as the Cromwell IV.

During the Cromwell's production run, six hull types (A–F) were used, each with different features. Early Cromwell IVs incorporated one of the last four variants (types C–F) with each being riveted, and incorporating minor changes related to armour, hatches, periscopes and the like. Later vehicles had welded hulls (types D–F, which also included the previous riveted runs) that featured similar modifications. To address various combat needs the Cromwell design branched to include the Cromwell VI close-support vehicle armed with a 95mm howitzer. Other variants included artillery observation, armoured recovery and dozer vehicles. A command version (brigade and divisional level), and a control equivalent (regimental level) were provided with additional radios.

JAGDPANZER IV

ORIGINS

Between 1939 and 1941 Germany's well-led and -motivated armed forces (the Wehrmacht) successfully employed mixed-asset and armoured formations and tactical air support in a string of battlefield successes, often against superior numbers and better-quality opponents. Intent on continuing the fight against the Soviet Union to capture vital resources, colonize territory and eliminate the threat of a potential Eastern Front, the Germans were surprised to encounter the Red Army's well-armed, armoured and manoeuvrable T-34 and 'heavy' KV-1 tanks in mid-1941. The Germans scrambled to develop an effective response, including upgrading the heavy, pre-war Tiger I design and creating a completely new medium tank, the Panther. Hitler's initial belief in a quick victory over the Soviets meant AFV production had not kept up with battlefield losses. Although mating captured or obsolete tank chassis with larger-calibre guns in fixed, open housings resulting in ad hoc *Panzerjäger* (armour hunter) vehicles had proven successful as a mobile anti-tank asset, long-term, purpose-built

As both sides fed reinforcements into the Normandy fighting, in late June 1944 9. SS-Panzer-Division *Hohenstaufen* was inserted west of Caen. Here, an *SS-Oberscharführer* and one of his SS-Sturmgeschütz-Abteilung 9 crewmates pose with their StuG III. While these early-war, short-barrelled *Sturmgeschütze* ('assault guns') were designated as 'assault artillery' and tasked with providing direct infantry support, later longer-barrelled versions, such as this example, proved excellent anti-tank assets, and often replaced tanks lost through attrition. Technically part of the artillery, *Sturmgeschütze* were commonly organized into battalions and allocated to Panzer divisions, in addition to being organic to those of the infantry. Reflecting their continuing status as artillerymen, assault-gun crews wore a 'Panzer wrap' tunic that buttoned along the wearer's right instead of in the middle, as with other armoured-vehicle personnel. As a continuation of early-war camouflage smocks the SS helped promote, these Dot 44 *Erbsenmuster* ('peas pattern') tunic and trouser uniforms comprised a mottled mix of three green and two brown colours. As this pattern was only used with uniforms, the two *Feldmütze* caps are a flat grey. (Bundesarchiv Bild 146-1989-113-19 Foto: Woscidio, Wilfried)

solutions were needed to streamline logistics, parts, training and maintenance, and to fight competitively in an increasingly attritional war. With the turretless, cost-effective Sturmgeschütz (StuG) III, a PzKpfw III derivative, having been upgraded from a short-barrelled infantry-support assault gun to a long 7.5cm StuK 40 L/43, from September 1942 a successful pattern was established in which both German and Soviet militaries would similarly modify and improve existing tank chassis to maintain a battlefield edge, however brief.

In late September 1942 the Heereswaffenamt (Army Weapons Office) ordered the creation of a more powerful self-propelled gun to supplant the StuG III assault gun. The new AFV was to possess 100mm of frontal armour and up to 50mm on the sides, wider tracks, 500mm ground clearance, a top speed of 26km/h and the lowest-possible firing position/profile. Under the Commander of the Replacement Army – a position subordinate to the Army Commander-in-Chief and OKH (Oberkommando des Heeres; Army High Command) – the arms inspectorates of the Heeresamt (General Army Office) then decided the new weapon system's organization, training structure and specifications. Under Oberst Friedrich-Wilhelm Holzhäuer's Waffenprüfungsamt (Weapons Proving Office), which was responsible for armoured forces, tanks, tank guns and *Panzerjäger*, these requirements were then sent to the Heereswaffenamt for formulating the technical specifications. If approved, they were then forwarded to the designated contractor/manufacturer to flesh out the design. To gain accurate and timely feedback on a vehicle's performance in the field from which to institute improvements or corrections, production and development personnel would commonly interview front-line crews and their officers after actions. As this new *Panzerjäger* was to incorporate the Panther's 7.5cm L/70 cannon within an enclosed, armoured superstructure, the stress imparted on the PzKpfw III chassis was considered too great and the more robust PzKpfw IV Ausf F was to be used instead. Hitler was shown the plans of the latest 'Sturmgeschütz auf Fahrgestell Pz.Kpfw.IV mit 7,5cm Kw.K 42 L/70' on 2 October 1942. This tank destroyer had thicker armour compared

Essentially obsolete by 1939, many German PzKpfw I and II tanks were subsequently transformed into ad hoc *Panzerjäger* to provide a mobile, armoured anti-tank option to extend their otherwise limited combat effectiveness. By removing the turrets from older tanks – whether domestically manufactured or captured – comparatively more powerful cannon types could be mounted to the chassis, albeit with limited traverse and open-topped superstructures. Improved *Panzerjäger* were fielded on the Eastern Front, including the Marder I (combining the German 7.5cm PaK 40 gun with the French Lorraine L37 tracked vehicle) and Marder II (mounting the Soviet 7.62cm or German PaK 40 on the PzKpfw II chassis). To repurpose the ageing, Czech-built PzKpfw 38(t), the Marder II's armament was used in the resulting Marder III. Although the makeshift *Panzerjäger* design offered tactical improvements over towed anti-tank guns, the vehicle's profile remained largely unchanged and its thinly armoured superstructure exposed its crews to small-arms fire and shrapnel from the top or rear. During the Normandy campaign PzJgLeAbt 130 had two Marder III Ausf M tank destroyers, such as the one shown here. (© IWM STT 7224)

to its predecessors, but as the 70-calibre gun was unavailable the shorter, less powerful 7.5cm PaK 39 L/43 was incorporated into pre-production vehicles, officially designated 'Jagdpanzer IV Ausf F für 7,5-cm PaK 39', or simply 'Panzerjäger 39'.

DEVELOPMENT

In contrast to American and British car and aircraft engine manufacturers that produced variations for tank use, the German firm, Maybach, focused specifically on producing tank engines. As with most AFV producers that had prior experience manufacturing heavy commercial equivalents, such as locomotives, VOMAG (Vogtländische Maschinenfabrik AG) had built lorries at Plauen, Saxony since 1915. Since 1941 the firm had also provided conversions for existing AFVs, while continuing to build lorries and buses until 1942. With Hitler having been shown plans for the proposed Jagdpanzer IV mounting the 7.5cm KwK 42 L/70 main gun on 2 October 1942, Vomag representatives presented him with a wooden mock-up on 14 May 1943. Now designated 'kleiner Panzerjäger und Panzerjäger der Fa. Vomag', several other, often equally wordy, names were used throughout its development and production. Following the battle of Kursk in July–August 1943, between 19 and 22 August Hitler received reports that in certain circumstances StuG IIIs had outperformed the PzKpfw IV in anti-tank actions, adding impetus to the proposal to halt production of the PzKpfw IV by late 1944 to focus instead on turretless alternatives, although this never occurred.

Before his retirement to reserve status on 24 September 1942, OKH chief-of-staff Generaloberst Franz Halder had called for the production Jagdpanzer IV to weigh no more than 35 tonnes, possess the highest-possible muzzle velocity, and use fixed projectiles that were small enough to be stored in quantity. The vehicle should also be

In late 1943 Vomag produced a soft-steel Jagdpanzer IV prototype (V-1), which unlike the production versions had a differently shaped mantlet and a rounded front plate. Instead of having a secondary weapon, this vehicle had matching pistol ports on either side of the main gun, with each having a conical cover that could be slid away to expose the opening. (© IWM STT 6607N)

no more than 6.2m long and 2.9m wide to allow for rail transport, and be less than 2.9m high to present a low profile. Having gained the Führer's approval to produce Jagdpanzer IV prototypes, in September 1943 Vomag commenced work on two such '0-Series' examples, with rounded front plate sides, a single driver periscope, and a 7.5cm Pak 39 L/43 gun. Although its sloped armour plate presented no compromising shot traps that could deflect an incoming projectile into the vehicle's thinner horizontal plates, during 1943 the design was incrementally improved. A soft-steel prototype (V-1) was completed on 20 October, and two months later it was shown to Hitler, who subsequently approved its production. The change from a turret to a superstructure led to the Jagdpanzer IV's internal components being rearranged from the configuration of the PzKpfw IV, including the fighting compartment's heater, radio, fuel tanks and ammunition racks.

By the end of 1943, Germany had a desperate need for AFVs of all types. Minister of Armaments and War Production Albert Speer's programme of mass production and rationalization was beginning to show signs of success. There was little room for delays, however, so with the exception of special programmes, such as the Panther and Tiger projects, any major industrial retooling was to be avoided. In January 1944 a second soft-steel Jagdpanzer IV prototype, V-2, was created that included a muzzle brake, rounded superstructure edges, a 7.92mm MG 42 machine gun at the gunner's position, and an Sfl ZF 1a targeting 'scope. This 'Panzerjäger 39 Test Series' prototype was subsequently provided for front-line service, with the side pistol loopholes and third periscope opening in the roof welded shut. By 1944 Speer's Ministry of Armaments and War Production had facilitated the dispersal of German industry to counter Allied strategic bombing, and increasingly controlled asset distribution to siphon resources to Party and Waffen-SS elements at the Army's expense. During trials, such as at Krupp's Meppen range, attending Heereswaffenamt personnel seldom consulted representatives from the firms or provided procedural details or test

JAGDPANZER IV (L/48) SPECIFICATIONS

General
Production run: January–November 1944 (11 months)
Vehicles produced: 769
Combat weight: 24,000kg
Crew: four (commander, gunner, loader/radio operator, driver)

Dimensions
Length (hull / overall): 5.90m / 6.85m
Width: 3.17m
Height: 1.86m

Armament
Main gun: 7.5cm PaK 39 L/48 (79 rounds)
Elevation: -8 degrees to +15 degrees
Traverse: 12 degrees left, 15 degrees right
Sight: Sfl ZF 1a (5×, 8 degrees)
Secondary: 1×7.92mm MG 42 (1,200 rounds)

Armour (degrees from vertical)
Glacis (upper / lower): 60mm @ 45 degrees / 50mm @ 55 degrees
Hull side: 30mm @ 0 degrees
Hull rear (upper / lower): 22mm @ 10 degrees / 22mm @ 10 degrees
Hull roof: 20mm @ 89 degrees
Hull bottom (front / rear): 12mm + 10mm @ 90 degrees / 10mm @ 90 degrees
Mantlet (outer / inner): 80mm curved / 80mm curved
Superstructure front: 60mm @ 50 degrees
Superstructure side (forward / rear): 30mm @ 30 degrees / 5mm @ 30 degrees
Superstructure rear (upper): 30mm @ 33 degrees
Superstructure roof (forward / rear): 20mm @ 0 degrees / 10mm @ 88 degrees
Superstructure bottom: 10mm @ 90 degrees
Skirting plate: 6mm @ 0 degrees

Communications
Internal: Bordsprechanlage B intercom
External: FuG 5 SE10U and a 10 WSa or 10 WSb 10-watt transmitter/USW receiver (wireless-telegraphy and radio-telephony stationary ranges were 6km and 4km, respectively)

Motive power
Engine: Maybach HL 120 TRM 60-degree 12-cylinder (water-cooled) 11.9l (petrol; optimally 74 octane)
Power to weight (sustained): 265bhp (198kW) @ 2,600rpm (11bhp (8.2kW)/tonne)
Transmission: Krupp-Wilson ZF Aphon SSG 76; six forward, one reverse
Fuel capacity: 470l in three tanks

Performance
Ground pressure: 0.86kg/cm²
Maximum speed (max / road / cross-country): 40km/h / 25km/h / 18km/h
Operational range (road / cross-country): 210km / 130km
Fuel consumption (road / cross-country): 0.45km/l / 0.28km/l
Fording: 1m
Step climbing: 0.6m
Climbing (ascending / descending): 30 degrees / 40 degrees
Trench crossing: 2.2m
Ground clearance: 0.4m

1.86m

3.17m

JAGDPANZER IV (L/48), 1./SS-PzJgAbt 12

The Jagdpanzer IV, like other German AFVs of the period, had a primer coat of RAL 8012 (red-brown), with those of Panzerjäger-Lehr-Abteilung 130 and SS-Panzerjäger-Abteilung 12 having an RAL 7028/1 (dark yellow) base colour. Panzerjäger-Lehr-Abteilung 130 incorporated a pattern of RAL 6003 (olive green) and RAL 8017 (red-brown), and used the typical three-digit numbering system (painted black with white borders on the superstructure sides), indicating the vehicle, platoon and company, with a *Balkenkreuz* displayed further back. SS-Panzerjäger-Abteilung 12's Jagdpanzer IVs were sprayed with RAL 7028/1, over which RAL 6003 was applied, although they seemed to lack vehicle numbering or national insignia. Both units' Jagdpanzer IVs were also covered with factory-applied *Zimmerit* anti-magnetic paste.

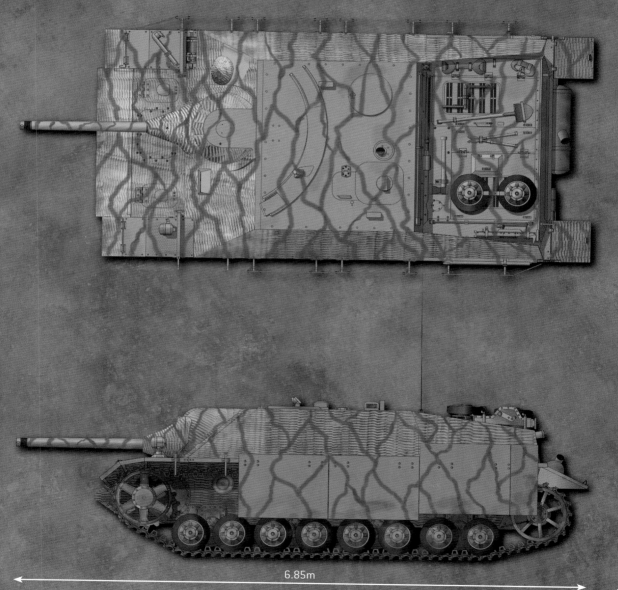

6.85m

With the Jagdpanzer IV (L/48)'s lengthy main gun overhang, placing spare tracks on the superstructure's upper rear helped balance the vehicle's centre of gravity. (© IWM STT 7135)

objectives. After the firms were satisfied with a vehicle's testing, the findings were sent to the Heereswaffenamt in Berlin, which carried out its own trials, such as at Kummersdorf for AFVs, before the vehicle was accepted for production. The Ministry of Armaments and War Production subsequently made decisions based on actual and estimated industry needs.

PRODUCTION

To provide the necessary manufacturing assets, Krupp-Gruson AG plant ceased PzKpfw IV production to manufacture its *Panzerjäger* variant, commencing in January 1944. Changes were frequently incorporated into the Jagdpanzer IV (L/48) during its production run, including the planned round machine-pistol ports for both hull sides being removed in favour of a rotating, roof-mounted Nahverteidigungswaffe (Close-in defensive weapon) for launching 9.2cm Schnellnebelkerze 39 smoke grenades, or projectiles fired from a standard (Leuchtpistole) or rifled (Kampfpistole) flare/signal pistol. As this weapon remained unavailable in sufficient quantities, a round armour plate cover with four screws was used to cover the opening on most vehicles. To simplify assembly, improve quality control and reduce manufacturing time and costs, the curved frontal armour was replaced by all-flat plates in production Jagdpanzer IVs. Because of the main gun's considerable overhang, spare track links that had been located on the glacis were refitted to the rear, while two spare road wheels were similarly moved to new brackets on the engine's port compartment cover.

During March 1944 the front superstructure's port machine-gun opening was covered, as without a dedicated crew member its use and value was minimal. Since the

opening had already been created, 60mm-thick conical plate was welded over it until an entirely solid replacement could be manufactured. Some Jagdpanzer IVs produced in March and April 1944 had an experimental mount for the *Rundumsfeuer* (all-around-fire) machine gun ahead of the gunner's visor. In April the lower corners of the inner weapon mount attachment were removed to reduce weight, and an improved main-gun recoil cylinder was developed. Starting in May 1944 the vehicle's front armour was thickened to 80mm, and the conical cover's diameter was enlarged for the starboard bow machine gun, which aided the user's grip and ability to traverse the weapon. Those Jagdpanzer IV main guns produced in late May and early June were threaded for muzzle brakes, which would reduce recoil stress and vent propellant smoke to the sides, but the barrel's height of just 1.4m meant the surrounding terrain was considerably disrupted during firing, which risked throwing up sufficient dust and debris to expose the Jagdpanzer IV's location. With reports from the field indicating that crews correspondingly removed the muzzle brakes, as doing so had no impact on performance, the manufacturer ceased adding them to the L/48 starting in May 1944. A new ball mantlet with rounded base plate was also incorporated, as was a Sternantenne D for command variants. During the spring of 1944, Vomag ceased producing the PzKpfw IV in favour of the Jagdpanzer IV to increase output. To simplify production, in June 1944 the formerly angled sides of the armoured cover over the coolant filler in the engine compartment cover were reconfigured as rectangular. Between the start of production in January 1944 and D-Day, 580 Jagdpanzer IVs had been ordered, but due to production problems between February and April, and aerial bombing of the vehicle's supplying firms in May, 466 were actually accepted.

A Jagdpanzer IV (L/48) adjacent to a later-model Panther Ausf A, with a ball machine-gun mount. Given that the *Panzerjäger's* port side cover is welded closed and it retains its muzzle brake, this vehicle was produced between March and May 1944. While the Panther's lengthy 70-calibre cannon contributed to its high muzzle velocity and considerable effective engagement range, it was a notable liability when traversing the turret in the very restrictive *bocage* (hedgerow) terrain found throughout most of Normandy. To help keep the overhang from damaging its alignment and elevation and traverse mechanisms during vehicle movement, the Panther was provided with a barrel lock, something the Jagdpanzer IV (L/48) lacked (it would be added to the later Jagdpanzer IV/70(A) and (V) variants). (© IWM STT 6600)

TECHNICAL SPECIFICATIONS

ARMAMENT

CROMWELL

Although the 6-pdr had been intended as an anti-tank gun, and was mounted in the Cromwell I–III, the General Staff wished to provide a more competitive and powerful weapon, while not unduly impacting existing manufacturing, especially as the rapidly outdated 2-pdr cannon then in use could fire armour-piercing ammunition only. By 1941, however, the need for a larger, dual-purpose piece that could also fire high explosive had gained impetus. A 1942 Army report compounded the problem of being outclassed by stating that British 75mm tank armaments were sufficient against contemporary German armour, although rapid German improvements required to maintain competitiveness with the Soviets were seemingly missed by the British. Although the Cromwell was originally to use the Vickers-Armstrong Ltd 75mm HV cannon, which was designed for an external mantlet, its recoil was too long for use within a turret intended to use an internal type, such as on the Cromwell; but with the company already developing a 75mm ROQF cannon that took 6-pdrs already mounted in British tanks, bored them out and inserted a new liner that was also re-drilled and subsequently rifled, the time, cost and effort involved in integrating a new system, such as the 75mm HV, could be avoided.

From late 1942, with the British Army increasingly using the M4 Sherman medium tank, which the Royal Ordnance Factory leveraged by adapting the US

CROMWELL AMMUNITION

Like its M72 predecessor, the M61 (**1**), an APCBC-T shell, had a relatively blunt ogive to offer the best penetration characteristic against most armour compositions and angles. Although more pointed projectiles achieved better success against softer plate that was thinner than the round's diameter at slower speeds, the chance for a ricochet or disintegration was increased. To improve aerodynamics, a thin, forged-steel-alloy ballistic cap ('windshield'), with a hard outside enclosing a relatively soft core, was placed over the shell proper, which also reduced impact stress. Although the round was manufactured with a hollowed base section to accommodate an explosive charge, British crews often removed the base section (and tracer) to avoid the possibility of premature detonation and improve flight stability even though its absence reduced the shell's penetrative capability.

The M48 (**2**), an HE projectile, incorporated an M48 fuse providing a super-quick impact option for use against enemy in the open that post-firing centrifugal force set for safety. A 0.05-second delay was also available for other soft targets, which even if not selected was activated to prevent duds should the M24 detonator fail on striking the target. The round had a bursting-charge mix of 0.05kg of TNT and 0.62kg of Amatol, and could be mated to one of three cartridges providing commensurate range changes, including Super (0.88kg, 14,000m), Normal (0.48kg, 11,400m) and Reduced (0.17kg, 7,200m). The lettering on

the shell included '75 G' (cannon calibre and type), 'TNT' (filler type), 'SHELL M48' (shell model) and '+' (weight-zone marking).

The following table presents the penetration (in millimetres) of Rolled Homogeneous Armour (RHA) at 0 degrees. Although these figures are derived from Allied and German testing documentation of the era, they cannot be considered completely accurate due to deviations in plate manufacturing and composition, penetration criteria and ammunition quality.

Ammunition penetration statistics, 75mm RQQF Mk V/VA					
	100m	500m	1,000m	1,500m	2,000m
M61 (APCBC-T) 6.8kg; 618m/sec	91	84	75	67	61
M48 (HE) 6.3kg; 463m/sec	8	8	8	8	8

tank's M3 breech to continue using its larger projectile, thus maintaining comparable ballistics but with less chamber pressure, the resulting 75mm cannon was used in the Cromwell IV. Designated 'Quick Fire' (QF), the cannon used single-piece rounds that included the shot/shell and cartridge propellant. During the Cromwell's production 60 per cent of the tanks were to mount the 75mm cannon, while 19 per cent were to be close-support tanks armed with the 95mm howitzer, with the remainder retaining the unmodified 6-pdr. Lacking the need for the front-wheel-drive M4 Sherman's obtrusive lateral driveshaft and being fitted entirely between the tracks, British tank hulls tended to possess a comparatively lower centre of gravity and improved cross-country performance. This configuration limited turret-ring diameters, and thus main armaments, however – something the Americans, Germans and Soviets tended to avoid by having the upper hull extend over the running gear to provide greater area.

One 7.92×57mm air-cooled, gas-operated Besa machine gun was mounted coaxially in the turret, with a second in the hull. Based on a Czech infantry design, this reliable, accurate machine gun could fire 450–550rd/min for normal use and 750–850rd/min during battlefield emergencies. It possessed an 823m/sec muzzle velocity and range out to some 450m. While firing the main gun was discouraged during movement, as it degraded accuracy, the hull machine gun commonly provided suppressing fire. It was effective against infantry and soft targets and used armour-piercing, ball, incendiary and tracer bullets from non-disintegrating, 225-round steel belts. A flash suppressor minimized visual exposure during firing, and a quick-change barrel helped avoid overheating from prolonged operation. The weapon also had a 'differential system' recoiling barrel that buffered the bolt during use and correspondingly reduced weapon and mounting stress.

JAGDPANZER IV

Compared to a tank, the lack of a complex and costly, protruding turret meant that self-propelled guns such as the Jagdpanzer IV could exploit their smaller profile to incorporate comparatively thicker armour and a heavier, more powerful main armament, while retaining a comparable weight. In concert with a muzzle brake and internal recoil cylinders, the vehicle's fixed-casemate superstructure also helped distribute the force of firing the main gun. Although the 7.5cm PaK 39 L/43 gun was incorporated into the prototype vehicles, the barrel's progressive rifling produced a similar effect to the added power generated by smaller guns that tapered at the bore. As the 7.5cm projectiles could also be used with the simpler, continuous rifling L/48 version mounted in the smaller Hetzer *Panzerjäger*, without changes to propellant charges, the L/48 was used on the first 769 production Jagdpanzer IVs. This change also reduced maintenance, as L/43 barrels wore out comparatively more quickly, with a 6,000-round life expectancy.

Having extensive experience as an arms manufacturer, Rheinmetall-Borsig AG (Unterlüß) and machinery producer Seitz-Werke GmbH (Bad Kreuznach) began production of the 7.5cm PaK 39 L/48 in 1943. Because the main gun's lateral movement was limited, hand wheels were sufficient for traverse and elevation. As the weapon's

A Jagdpanzer IV (L/48) minus its muzzle brake. Note the spare tracks on the superstructure's rear, and the brackets for mounting *Schürzen* armour plates to counter shaped-charge weapons, such as the American Bazooka. (© IWM STT 7134)

1   2   3   4   5

JAGDPANZER IV AMMUNITION

The Pzgr Patr 39 KwK 40 (**1**), an APCBC-HE projectile, included a cap to assist off-angle penetration and a ballistic cap to improve aerodynamics and accuracy. It used a BdZ 5103 or BdZ 5103* (tracer) base fuse to detonate an 18g explosive filler of RDX/wax (90:10) to improve post-impact damage, and a 2.41kg propelling charge of Digl R P G1. The Pzgr Patr 40 KwK 40 (**2**), an APCR round, incorporated a tungsten-carbide core, but lacked an explosive filler and fuse. It had a 2.2kg Gu R P 7.7 propelling charge.

Although the 7.5cm cannon could fire the shaped-charge Gr 38 HI/B KwK 40 (**3**) HEAT round – and the HI/C – the scarcity of these projectiles meant that the Jagdpanzer IV was unlikely to have used either in Normandy. The Sprgr Patr 34 KwK 40 (**4**), an HE projectile, used a klAZ 23 nose fuse to detonate 0.66kg of amatol (40/60 bursting charge) on impact. It used a 2.2kg propelling charge of Gu R P 7.7. The 7.5cm Nbgr (**5**), a smoke round, used a klAZ 23 Nb fuse to trigger a small picric-acid burster charge to dispense an 80/20 oleum/pumice smoke mix.

The following table presents the penetration (in millimetres) of RHA at 0 degrees and at 30 degrees (the two penetrations separated by a forward slash).

Ammunition penetration statistics, 7.5cm PaK 39 L/48					
	100m	500m	1,000m	1,500m	2,000m
Pzgr Patr 39 KwK 40 (APCBC-HE) 6.80kg; 750m/sec	135/106	123/96	109/85	97/74	86/64
Pzgr Patr 40 KwK 40 (APCR) 4.15kg; 990m/sec	176/143	154/120	130/97	109/77	92/NA
Gr 38 HI/B KwK 40 (HEAT) 4.57kg; 450m/sec	80/75	80/75	80/75	80/75	80/75
Sprgr Patr 34 KwK 40 (HE) 5.74kg; 550m/sec	8/NA	8/NA	8/NA	8/NA	8/NA

firing lever was adjacent to the traverse wheel, the proximity enabled the gunner to reposition towards and engage a new target quickly. The main gun's semi-automatic sliding block ejected a spent cartridge, and was ready for firing as soon as the next round was inserted. The main gun's relatively high velocity and flat trajectory also increased accuracy at longer ranges and minimized the effects of wind drift and trunnion cant, in which a lateral firing angle imparted a sideways movement along the round's trajectory.

To provide localized firepower the Jagdpanzer IV possessed an MG 42 machine gun, which could fire 1,200 rounds per minute, thereby risking the consumption of considerable amounts of 7.92mm ammunition; an undisciplined operator could go through a 250-round belt in just 12 seconds. Sustained firing was frowned upon due to barrel overheating and unnecessary wear. In March and early April 1944 a roof mount was added to accommodate the weapon for remote-controlled use. A close-defence weapon set at 30 degrees on the roof could be rotated 360 degrees to launch the roughly 16 2.6cm smoke cartridges or explosive shells.

ARMOUR

CROMWELL

While pre-1939 British industry advances in metallurgy promoted much stronger welding options compared to riveting, which had originated with the production of high-pressure boilers, welding was not used on a British tank until the Cromwell. In 1936 the English Steel Corporation began integrating a higher percentage of chromium-molybdenum to produce 'Hykro' tank steel armour that produced less impact-related spalling and had a better tensile-strength range compared to other alloys. Only the front and rear hull plates were welded on to the side plates using angle brackets, which were riveted for additional robustness. Having stopped high-explosive bomb production to focus on making iron and non-ferrous castings for its commercial vehicles, Leyland Motors employed large jigs and rotary manipulators for final assembly and subassemblies to produce welded tank hulls and turrets.

In June 1942 the Department of Tank Design asked Leyland Motors to produce several welded hulls of the Centaur III and Centaur IV type to assess the merits of such efforts against riveted construction to determine whether man-hours could be reduced, and field maintenance improved. Finding welding to be superior in that it also permitted stronger plate equivalents, the Armoured Fighting Vehicle Liaison

Committee determined in November 1942 that the process should be applied to the Cromwell. That month the Ministry of Supply ordered Leyland Motors to produce three welded hulls based on the latter's drawing-office design. In July 1943 Leyland Motors' fully welded Centaur front plates better resisted impacts than riveting, and three months later the company transitioned to producing the Cromwell, with a fully welded front. The shortage of skilled labour and welding experience, however, prevented armour manufacturers from completing the various production programmes envisaged or desired.

Despite pressure to reduce the use of scarce non-ferrous metals such as nickel, molybdenum and chromium, strict British production controls usually meant reductions in armour quality were avoided even though almost all of it was manufactured using the open-hearth method, which impeded quality control. With armour hardness dependent primarily on the alloy and heat treatment, rolling reduced grain size, and added direction to promote structural strength. The Cromwell's armour predominantly comprised machineable-quality plates greater than 15mm ('I.T.80' – an Izod Test designation indicating the level of impact resistance), which did not necessitate the use of specialized cutting tools. Its thinner equivalent engine deck and hull floor front were designated 'I.T.100', with the hull floor reinforced with 'I.T.120' plate to increase protection against mines. 12.7mm of heat-treated carbon-manganese steel backing plate ('I.T.110') provided the base plate for the turret's floor, as well as its front, sides and rear over which thicker 'I.T.80' plate was bolted. The vehicle's hull plates were entirely welded, with the upper chassis and turret a mix of welding and riveting, in which a hard outer plate was bolted to a softer inner one – a combination that offered less protection than a single piece. British armour plate was essentially equivalent to US armour plate in its resistance to penetrations, but its quality was more variable, and some Cromwells contended with substandard plate due to manufacturing inexperience.

A captured Jagdpanzer IV is depicted in this photo, taken on 24 August 1944. The arm insignia indicates civilian War Department employees. The men were tasked with inspecting the European Theater of Operations to help determine the battlefield effectiveness of American equipment and weapons. Produced by Chemische Werke Zimmer AG (Berlin), the *Zimmerit* anti-magnetic paste covering much of the vehicle comprised a mixture of sawdust, glue, non-combustible fillers and a dark-yellow pigment that was spread over the desired area (usually at the factory) using trowels and blowtorches and allowed to dry. The material provided a barrier that was sufficiently thick to negate a magnetic mine's magnetostatic field. (US Army Signal Corps ETO HQ 44 12289)

JAGDPANZER IV

To best withstand a variety of impacting projectiles and blast damage, cast and Rolled Homogeneous Armour (RHA) plate required hardness and tensile (stretching) strength. Germany's increasing shortage of key elements necessary for producing impact-resistant steel, disruptions from enemy aerial bombing and quality-control issues and sabotage due to the large number of unskilled forced labourers that were used to free German workers for military service meant that every effort was made to maintain quality using low-alloy equivalents if necessary. Such high-strength, low-alloy steel comprised carbon (less than 0.5 per cent) and manganese (1–3 per cent). What face-hardening that had been done on the PzKpfw IV remained, which proved effective against uncapped anti-tank rounds by promoting ricocheting or shattering due to such hard, tapered-nose projectiles lacking the means to correct off-angle impacts. In contrast, comparatively 'softer' RHA defeated rounds by absorbing the strike and dissipating its energy. As one of several metallurgical impact-resistance tests, Brinell Hardness Scale values (Brinell Hardness Numbers) under 375 were considered 'machineable quality', in which armour could be machined without losing integrity, and was reasonably able to resist repeated strikes without undue spalling or cracking. Values greater than this proved brittle and lost resistance, especially against overmatching rounds whose diameter measurements exceeded that of the plate's thickness.

Unlike the earlier makeshift Marder *Panzerjäger*, with their open superstructures that exposed the crew to weather and enemy fire, the Jagdpanzer IV was completely enclosed. Although this reduced visibility, the design produced a much stronger, purpose-built framework. Initially, German developers believed that 80mm of glacis plate set at 45 degrees would provide sufficient resistance to American 75mm and British 17-pdr tank rounds at most engagement ranges. In February 1943 the Heereswaffenamt suggested that a greater angle was needed, but due to the delays such a change would likely have on production the idea was rejected. For Jagdpanzer IV production vehicles the upper glacis was 60mm thick and remained at 45 degrees, while the lower 50mm plate was angled to 55 degrees, which equated to an equivalent horizontal thickness of 85mm and 61mm, respectively.

Having retained the PzKpfw IV's welded hull, Böhler AG (Kapfenberg) and Vítkovice Ironworks (Ostrava), the latter with its own coal mine and coking plant, produced the Jagdpanzer IV's interlocking and welded steel superstructure plates. To strengthen the Jagdpanzer IV's most likely enemy facing, its front and glacis comprised interlocking plates, while the use of periscopes rather than vision slits helped maintain plate integrity and strength, especially as plate thicknesses continually increased. The superstructure was bolted through angle sections to the lower hull, with its sloping sides extending over the tracks, which increased internal space. To protect against hand-placed magnetic mines, *Zimmerit* anti-magnetic paste was factory-applied to vehicles, while spaced 5mm plates were bolted to brackets that had been welded to the superstructure's side. By prematurely detonating shaped-charge projectiles fired by weapons such as the American Bazooka and British PIAT, the effect of their directed molten jets would be disrupted and degraded when they reached the vehicle armour. The main gun was offset 200mm right of centre, and located within a mount comprising a specially designed cast *Topfblende* ('pot diaphragm'), behind which an 80mm curved housing and an equally thick mask kept the gun off the floor, thereby eliminating what was often a complicated floor mechanism found in other assault guns. Although this configuration was more expensive to produce than similar designs, such as the *Walzenblende* ('roller mount') on the Panther and Soviet ISU-152, and the *Kugelblende* ('ball mount') on the SU-85 and SU-100, it provided greater protection.

MOBILITY

CROMWELL

The driver's compartment included a large gear lever projecting from the floor up to between his knees, with steering levers to the outside that acted on the differential to slow one side and speed the other up to enable turn. A handbrake lever was located against the right bulkhead, with clutch, brake and accelerator pedals on the floor. For adaptation as the Meteor 4B, the 1,000bhp (746kW) V12 27-litre Merlin engine was stripped of its supercharger, reduction gear and other components, which reduced its power to a more manageable 600bhp (447kW), and made it more compact and easier to produce. Several changes, such as modifying the fan drive, having a full-flow oil filter, increasing the oil pump's capacity and modifying its magneto advance increased the Meteor engine's power to its final output of roughly 650bhp (485kW). The engine was located between the vehicle's two air filters and two fuel tanks, and when the main engine was off, an innovative Morris auxiliary motor charged the batteries and powered

the radios, turret traverse and gun-control equipment. The auxiliary motor also powered a 'boiling vessel' on which food or water could be heated. The main engine connected to a starter motor that penetrated the rear firewall and into the fighting compartment. An independent charging set engine was positioned left of the main engine, which powered the generator and ventilator fan.

The Meteor engine's power was transferred to a triple dry-plate clutch, and then to a rear-mounted Merritt-Brown Z.5 gearbox, with five forward and one reverse (12km/h) gears. As a controlled-differential steering system two inner steering brakes on either side would lock their respective idler pinions inside the housing to enable turning. Outside of this, brake wheels connected to their respective final drives against the hull, and then to external drive sprockets. To prevent excessive heating on such a large vehicle the regenerative system avoided any loss of power or speed during turns by forcing one half shaft to rotate slower than the other. This simple system provided maximum power transfer to increase torque and thus mobility over rough terrain. The Cromwell's Merritt-Brown transmission also allowed the vehicle to pivot in place when in neutral.

The Cromwell's suspension comprised six units, each having two pairs of road wheels connected via axle arms, and three concentric springs, with a shock absorber at the front and rear sections. Although the vehicle's improved Christie independent coil-spring design proved reliable, its road-wheel tyres were known to crumble under the vehicle's weight. To compensate for a shortage of spares, crews often cannibalized their Crusader anti-aircraft tanks, which meant that many Cromwells sported a mix of solid and perforated tyres. At 356mm wide, the vehicle's 126 webbed and spudded cast-steel tracks were an improvement over those of previous British tanks, with each set weighing 1,036kg. Reliability and power were Cromwell hallmarks, which translated into an impressive 23bhp/tonne (17.2kW/tonne), and a high speed that necessitated the engine be governed to avoid damaging the suspension.

JAGDPANZER IV

Although Generaloberst Halder once stated that the ideal *Panzerjäger* would have at least 14bhp/tonne (10.4kW/tonne), the Jagdpanzer IV managed just 11bhp/tonne (8.2kW/tonne). The Jagdpanzer IV retained the PzKpfw IV's chassis, power plant and suspension, with a driveshaft running under the fighting compartment that connected the engine with a three-plate clutch and the transmission. The rather complex Krupp-Wilson ZF Aphon SSG 76 synchromesh transmission had been incorporated into the PzKpfw III and PzKpfw IV, and included the steering mechanism and differential within one unit. Steering relied on a mechanical planetary gear and two levers operating brakes, where pulling one lever about one-third of its total movement operated a clutch and steering brake. When changing to a lower gear, double clutching was necessary to place the engine in neutral momentarily. To avoid undue resistance when ascending a steep slope, drivers were trained to avoid steering, if possible, and employ the same gear going down as up. A foot brake activated both sides simultaneously, although this could be avoided with the engine running at around 2,400rpm. As individual Jagdpanzer IVs risked damage to their transmissions when towing equivalently sized vehicles, it was preferable to use two such vehicles for the task, and then using crossed cables.

Since 1939 the Heer had chosen petrol for its tank engines, due to the fuel industry believing that replicating better-performing diesel synthetically would be problematic. Even though by 1942 the synthetic alternative was more abundant than originally anticipated, the Jagdpanzer IV remained petrol-powered, with two mechanical and one electric fuel pump. Maybach-Motorenbau GmbH (Friedrichshafen) provided a wide array of German AFV engines during the war, including the HL 120 TRM found in the PzKpfw IV Ausf F and the Jagdpanzer IV, while Auto-Union AG (Chemnitz) provided components. These vehicles were designed to operate on the Eastern Front and were equipped with a hot coolant system to assist starting in extreme cold. Whereas some German tank engines were air-cooled for colder climates, Speer's Tank Commission chairman, Gerd Stieler von Heydekampf, opted for a water-based equivalent, believing they were less bulky and complicated.

Starting the engine required a Bosch BNG 4/24 motor or the cranking of a flywheel. Two radiators were positioned astride the engine and helped maintain coolant temperature at around 80 degrees Celsius. The Jagdpanzer IV's three fuel-tank levels were coordinated, but the lack of an accurate gauge meant that the driver began looking to refuel once the final tank was activated. As was common with German AFVs, the emphasis was upon maximizing internal space at the expense of easy engine access. Although the Jagdpanzer IV lacked shock absorbers, its leaf-spring suspension, with eight rubberized rollers arranged on four bogie pairs, provided a stable ride. The PzKpfw IV's manoeuvrability issues resulting from narrow tracks and increasing vehicle weights continued with its *Panzerjäger* variant, which possessed 400mm-wide (including pins) Moorburger Trackenwerke (Hamburg) manganese tracks, with 99 links per side.

THE COMBATANTS

BRITISH AND POLISH TRAINING

For British tankers, basic training took place at the Primary Training Wing, Bovington Camp, Dorset for six weeks of 'square-bashing' in which precision marching was demanded, as well as polishing, drilling, running, and attending lectures on a range of military subjects. On completion of training the men were assigned to 58th (Young Soldiers) Training Regiment, Royal Armoured Corps (RAC) for the next six months, where they conducted additional physical training, route marches, and driving and maintenance instruction on various British tanks and lorries. Courses in gunnery and radio operation were also provided, with roughly one-quarter of intakes selected as possible officer material, and assigned additional related duties. At the end of training the men were deposited in an unknown field dozens of kilometres from base. Lacking money and food, groups of around half a dozen were expected to make their way back using a compass and map. On completing the assignment, a passing-out parade followed, which officially ended basic training.

During training for Normandy, much of the time was spent acclimating the crews to their new Cromwells, with many distrustful, having preferred to retain their familiar M4 Shermans, which were left in Italy. With the Germans having fielded their 56-tonne Tiger I, with its thick armour and 8.8cm cannon, during the fighting in Tunisia, many British tankers were concerned that their mounts were inferior, doubts that were only partially assuaged by the new British tank's considerable speed. After 7th Armoured Division elements conducted a week's gunnery practice and lorry maintenance at the Kirkcudbright Range in south-western Scotland, live-fire tank training commenced back at West Tofts (Thetford Forest) in Norfolk. Cromwell

A Sherman III of C Squadron, 4th CLY in Italy, 1943. Created on 3 September 1939 and assigned to Home Defence forces after Dunkirk, in August 1941 4th CLY was sent to North Africa to serve with 7th Armoured Division. In 1943, with the Normandy landing date approaching, the 'Desert Rats' seemed a natural choice to contribute badly needed armoured combat veterans to the British effort. In January 1944 the formation was withdrawn from the Mediterranean theatre (although its Shermans remained behind) and undertook four months of training in Norfolk. When 7th Armoured Division returned to Britain, for many of the men it was the first time in years that they had been home and several expressed dismay at being slated for additional combat when so many trained personnel had yet to be committed. Unlike its peer formations that employed the Cromwell in reconnaissance regiments only, 7th Armoured Division used the vehicle in its three armoured regiments. (© IWM NA 7862)

drivers were later sent to the Fighting Vehicle Proving Establishment at Longcross Halt Camp in Surrey to test their mounts. Some six weeks before D-Day 22nd Armoured Brigade focused on training in advancing to contact, halting and attacking; with some recent infantry–armour experience in Italy, artillery support, however good, was to be emphasized. Attacking fortified positions was not practised. With most training completed by April 1944, leave and recreation were arranged to improve morale.

Allied forces slated for the invasion conducted Exercise *Smash* on 18 April 1944 to help acclimate the participants, and test command and control, tactics and new equipment. For all of their beneficial realism and intensity, three of the four such exercises mounted occurred in good weather and calm seas, and overcast skies that limited Royal Air Force participation.

Polish training and organization were based on the British model, but with Brig Maczek leading, so many of his former subordinates, habits and practices learned in Polish basic and subsequent training naturally persisted. Highly motivated to fight the

A Cromwell V of No. 100 RAC OCTU (Officer Cadet Training Unit) at the Royal Military College, Sandhurst in Berkshire, 1944 (note the driver's rear-view mirror and turret aiming rods). (© IWM HU 99811)

Established in 1918, Poland's 10th Mounted Rifle Regiment served as cavalry during the Russo-Polish War (1919–21), including the pivotal battle of Radzymin (1920) that repelled a Soviet offensive to capture Warsaw. In 1938 the unit participated in Poland's annexation of Zaolzie from Czechoslovakia, and in September 1939 fought 2. Panzer-Division and 4. leichte Division in the Kraków region. Although 10th Mounted Rifle Regiment gave a good account of itself the combination of rapid German armoured thrusts and tactical air support, and the Soviet invasion in the east eliminated any hope of a Polish victory or tangible assistance from Britain or France. Following Poland's capitulation the regiment was interned in what was officially neutral Hungary. With thousands of Polish soldiers having escaped westwards to continue the fight a reconstituted 10th Mounted Rifle Regiment participated in the similarly brief French campaign. On France's surrender in May–June 1940 the unit once again dissolved and its members made their way to Britain, only to be re-formed there a third time. On 25 February 1942 Poland's 1st Armoured Division was formed, which included 10th Mounted Rifle Regiment. Shown here training with Crusader III tanks in 1943, the regiment would later be issued Cromwells prior to the Normandy campaign. The two closest tankers wear regimental badges commemorating their unit's formation, and Royal Armoured Corps crash helmets, which offered no ballistic protection, being predominantly pressed fibre. (© IWM HU 128267)

British and Polish unit organizations

On 10 June 1944, Lt-Col The Viscount Arthur Cranley's 4th CLY fielded 43 Cromwell IVs, 12 Fireflies, 11 Stuart III/Vs and 692 officers and men. Major H.C. Stockdale's regimental headquarters included four Cromwell IVs. A Squadron (acting Major Peter M.R. Scott) included a headquarters troop (one Cromwell IV and two Cromwell VIs) and Nos 1–4 troops (each with three Cromwell IVs and one Firefly). Captain Ian B. 'Ibby' Aird's B Squadron (HQ Troop plus Nos 5–8 troops) and Major Peter McColl's C Squadron (HQ Troop plus Nos 9–12 troops) were similarly outfitted. To provide organic support 4th CLY also possessed headquarters, intercommunications, administration, reconnaissance (11 Stuart IIIs) and anti-aircraft troops under a squadron command.

While 22nd Armoured Brigade lacked the 75mm Sherman and employed its Cromwells as main battle tanks, the Poles possessed both vehicle types and were organized along more typical British lines. As part of 1st Armoured Division, on 7 August 1944 Major Jan Maciejowski's 10th Mounted Rifle Regiment (686 officers and men) used its 53 Cromwell IVs for armoured reconnaissance duties. These were allocated to Captain of Cavalry Jerzy Wasilewski's 1st Squadron (squadron headquarters with two Cromwell IVs and two Cromwell VIs, and Nos 1–5 troops, each with three Cromwell IVs), and the identically outfitted 2nd Squadron (Captain of Cavalry Michał Gutowski; Nos 6–10 troops) and 3rd Squadron (Captain of Cavalry Herman Cieśliński; Nos 11–15 troops). The regimental HQ and Reconnaissance Platoon each possessed one Cromwell IV.

Germans and ultimately re-establish their nation, Polish forces were often used in shock roles, such as in Italy. Having remained in Scotland to train in Arbroath and later Haddington, both on the east coast, in May 1943, 10th Mounted Rifle Regiment relocated south to facilities in England, including Pickering, North Yorkshire and

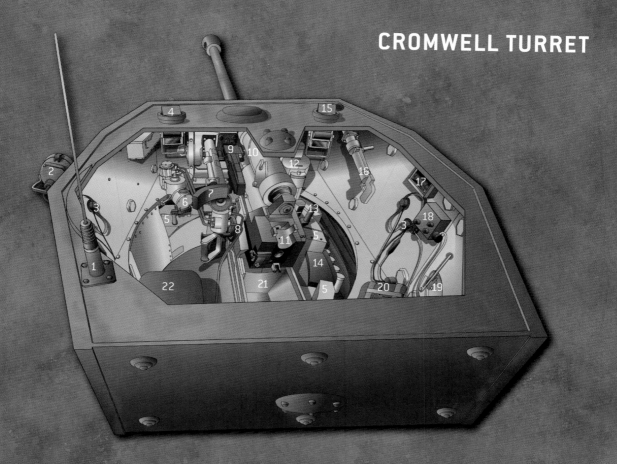

1. Aerial
2. Spotlight
3. No. 19 radio microphone headset
4. Gunner's Vickers Tank Periscope
5. Main gun ammunition storage
6. Turret traverse motor and handle
7. Gunner's No. 50×3 ML Mk II sighting telescope
8. Elevation wheel
9. Coaxial 7.92mm Besa machine gun
10. Main gun recoil cylinder
11. Main gun breech
12. Container for 2in smoke bombs
13. Breech handle
14. Loader's seat
15. Loader's Vickers Tank Periscope
16. 2in bomb thrower
17. Hellesen handlamp
18. No. 19 radio control box
19. Pistol port
20. Signal satchel
21. Spent cartridge bag
22. Gunner's seat

The Cromwell's divided forward section included hull positions for a driver (starboard), who accessed his position via a sliding roof hatch, and turned the vehicle using two steering columns, with each braking a different track. The driver could open a front aperture for better forward visibility, although this commonly funnelled dust and debris into the vehicle's interior. Both he and the adjacent co-driver/machine-gunner, who also 'lived downstairs', were consequently susceptible to conjunctivitis and other eye problems. The Cromwell's turret risked blocking the driver's hatch when traversed past 45 degrees from centre.

The vehicle's commander, gunner and loader/radio operator occupied a rather cramped central fighting compartment, which included the power-operated turret and an attached basket that ensured its contents rotated as a single unit. The gunner sat to the left of the breech, and operated the turret's rotation using hand and foot controls. The commander sat behind the gunner and was responsible for orchestrating the team, maintaining communication with his assigned troop, and allocating targets and ranges. The loader/radio operator sat to the right of the breech, and operated the vehicle's radios at the turret rear.

Having led the motorized 10th Cavalry Brigade (of which 10th Mounted Rifle Regiment was a part), after Poland's 1939 capitulation Stanisław Maczek entered Hungarian internment, but soon escaped to the west. He was placed in command of a re-formed and renamed 10th Armoured Cavalry Brigade during the 1940 French campaign; on its conclusion he dissolved the brigade and along with thousands of his countrymen made his way to the relative safety of Britain. For Maczek this involved travelling to French Algeria and then Morocco disguised as a Foreign Légionnaire, before sailing to neutral Portugal, and finally to Bristol, England on 21 September 1940. Although initially relegated to Scottish coastal defence duty, within two years Maczek had helped orchestrate the creation of Poland's 1st Armoured Division, to which he was assigned as divisional commander.

Throughout 1943 and early 1944 the formation trained for the Normandy invasion using several successive Allied tank types. With new Cromwell IV tanks having been issued to British armoured units starting in October 1943, Maj-Gen Maczek (left) appropriated one, nicknamed 'Hela', from which to exercise command effectively in the field. The vehicle's turret roof includes a circular ventilator that helped clear the turret of propellant smoke, which could quickly fill the interior and prevent the crew from performing their duties. (Czesław Datka/National Digital Archive, Poland/CC0 1.0)

Chippenham, Cambridgeshire. With strict security in place, units training in the latter area's relatively open terrain had no idea they were to operate in Normandy's dense *bocage* until just before D-Day. In September 1943, Polish 1st Armoured Division (including 10th Mounted Rifle Regiment) began reorganization to the most recent British war establishment comprising a single armoured brigade, an infantry brigade, and artillery and services. In late November 1943 the unit moved to Falkirk, midway between Glasgow and Edinburgh, where it was re-equipped and allocated new Cromwell tanks. Live-fire gunnery exercises followed at the Kirkcudbright range during which Polish 1st Armoured Division recorded the best results of all Allied armoured divisions conducting such exercises to date. That spring, 10th Mounted Rifle Regiment was deemed combat-ready and in mid-May 1944 was sent to Scarborough near Pickering in preparation for the invasion of France.

GERMAN TRAINING

By 1943 the shortage of experienced Panzerwaffe personnel prompted Generaloberst Heinz Guderian, Inspector General of Armoured Troops, to make the risky decision to provide a force tailored to eliminating the threat of invasion in the West. On 30 December 1943, with Hitler's approval, OKW (Oberkommando der Wehrmacht;

These Jagdpanzer IV/70(V)s and *Panzerfaust*-armed grenadiers are advancing to fight the advancing Red Army in Hungary in 1945. During March and April 1944 the newly created Panzer-Lehr-Division was abruptly relocated from its training areas near the French cities of Nancy and Verdun to Budapest to help bolster the faltering Axis Hungarian government now that Soviet forces had pushed into its eastern territory. During this period, Panzerjäger-Lehr-Abteilung 130 (formerly III./PzLeRgt 130) received replacements from Panzerjäger-Ersatz-Abteilung 43. In mid-March it accepted its authorized complement of 31 newly produced Jagdpanzer IVs, although they lacked sufficient replacement parts and equipment. (Bundesarchiv Bild 146-1976-039-09 Foto: Krumme)

High Command of the Armed Forces) officially sanctioned the Panzer-Lehr-Division's establishment, which gathered personnel from the combat-veteran instructors stationed at Panzertruppenschule I (Bergen), Panzertruppenschule II, Kommandostab (Krampnitz) and the Fahnenjunker Artillery School (Mourmelon), as well as existing combat or *Lehr* (demonstration) units, and from the Ersatzheer (Replacement Army). As a result of Guderian having recently stressed the importance of coalescing the Panzer-Lehr-Division's component elements into a powerful offensive force, on 5 February 1944 it entered a period of intensive training. To maximize the formation's strength and readiness, on 18 February 1944 Guderian decreed that training would cease only on his authority. With Bayerlein having fought Allied forces in North Africa, his training regimen reflected these experiences, such as familiarization with placing and breaching minefields, and practising twilight and night marches to avoid the anticipated Allied air dominance. Short-notice, formation-level training, river crossings, and live-fire exercises that often incorporated all of the division's combat elements were also stressed.

In Hungary, the Panzer-Lehr-Division (aka 130. Panzer-Division after 4 April 1944 due to many of its component units having that number designation) soon resumed training, which continued after the formation returned to France. Throughout May the division's staff officers war-gamed defensive options and reconnoitred the Atlantic Wall and approach routes from the Cotentin Peninsula to Le Havre. On 7 July 1944 the Panzer-Lehr-Division would be pulled from the Tilly-sur-Seulles area and sent west to help shore up the defence near Saint-Lô. Some two weeks later 116. Panzer-Division was similarly allocated to the threatened sector, with its Panzerjäger-Abteilung 228 (shown here) moving into assembly positions on 24 July. (Bundesarchiv Bild 101I-496-3464-06 Foto: Burchhaus)

German unit organizations

By 6 June 1944, 169 Jagdpanzer IVs had been allocated to various training facilities, independent units and organic *Panzerjäger* battalions within six Panzer and *Panzergrenadier* divisions in the West. Each *Panzerjäger* company was to receive either ten or 14 vehicles, as per KStN 1149 (Kriegstärkenachweisung; War Table of Organization). *Panzerjäger* battalions in Panzer divisions generally had two Jagdpanzer IV-armed companies, each of ten vehicles, and an additional Jagdpanzer IV for the battalion commander. *Panzergrenadier* divisions were to have two companies of 14 vehicles each, with three more for the battalion staff. (Both battalion types also fielded a third *Panzerjäger* company armed with towed weapons.) Production delays, breakdowns and other factors meant actual numbers of Jagdpanzer IVs available seldom equalled the official TOE. The values given below show the latter.

On 1 June 1944, Major Joachim Barth's Panzerjäger-Lehr-Abteilung 130 had a paper strength of 31 Jagdpanzer IVs and 513 officers and men. Its *Stabs-Kompanie* included four Jagdpanzer IVs, plus signals, anti-aircraft and combat-engineer platoons. The battalion fielded three companies led by Oberleutnant Werner Wagner (1./PzJgLeAbt 130), Hauptmann Pfender (2./PzJgLeAbt 130) and Hauptmann Julius Oventrop (3./PzJgLeAbt 130), each having three platoons with a full complement of three Jagdpanzer IVs each.

On 7 August 1944, SS-Sturmbannführer Hans-Jakob Hanreich's SS-Panzerjäger-Abteilung 12 fielded 21 Jagdpanzer IVs and 12 PaK 40s, with a paper complement of 516 officers and men. SS-Obersturmführer Georg Hurdelbrink's 1./SS-PzJgAbt 12 had its full complement of ten Jagdpanzer IVs, while SS-Obersturmführer Johann 'Hans' Wachter's 2./SS-PzJgAbt 12 possessed six vehicles, with the remainder undergoing minor repairs. SS-Hauptsturmführer Günther Wöst's 3./SS-PzJgAbt 12 fielded 12 'Maultier' ('Mule' half-track)-towed 7.5cm PaK 40 guns.

Pictured here on 17 June 1944, these *Hitlerjugend* soldiers have just been awarded Iron Crosses for bravery. Having decided to establish a combat division composed of Hitlerjugend (Hitler Youth) members, on 24 June 1943 Hitler officially ordered the formation's creation; it was primarily composed of teenagers born in 1926/27, with veteran officers and NCOs coming from 1. SS-Panzergrenadier-Division *Leibstandarte SS Adolf Hitler* or the Heer. With Hitler wishing to have I. SS-Panzerkorps comprise two Panzer divisions, *Hitlerjugend* was to be partnered with *Leibstandarte*. On 6 February 1944 the I. SS-Panzerkorps commander, Obergruppenführer und General der Waffen-SS Josef 'Sepp' Dietrich, ordered *Leibstandarte's* SS-Panzerjäger-Abteilung 1 personnel to be reassigned to *Hitlerjugend*. Ten days later the unit, by now redesignated SS-Panzerjäger-Abteilung 12, moved to its assigned quarters south-east of Antwerp, Belgium. In anticipation of the Allied invasion, on 5 April 1944 *Hitlerjugend* relocated to the Nogent-le-Roi area, some 90km south-west of Paris. Designated 12. SS-Panzer-Division *Hitlerjugend* on 22 October 1943, it was arrayed west of Caen on 6 June 1944. (Photo by ullstein bild/ullstein bild via Getty Images)

JAGDPANZER IV FIGHTING COMPARTMENT

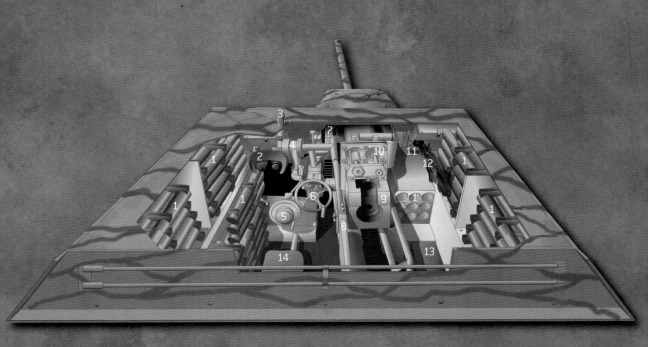

1. 7.5cm ammunition rack
2. SfI ZF 1a headrest
3. SfI ZF 1a periscope
4. SfI ZF 1a mount
5. Traverse wheel

6. Elevation wheel
7. Inner mantlet
8. Protective breech shield and bar
9. Main gun breech
10. Main gun recoil cylinder

11. Starboard pistol port
12. MG 42 machine gun
13. Loader's seat
14. Gunner's seat

The Jagdpanzer IV's crew included a forward-facing driver, gunner and commander situated in line along the port side, and a loader/radio operator opposite and facing the main gun that bisected the unheated fighting compartment. The driver had two vision slits in the glacis, but a blind spot existed to his right due to the main gun's housing. Such visibility limitations also hindered manoeuvring the vehicle over rugged or constricted terrain.

The Jagdpanzer IV's commander had three periscopes, including a rotatable episcope, a fixed Rundblickfehrnrohr Rbl F 3b, and a Scherenfernrohr SF 14 Z binocular rangefinder. In addition to feeding the main gun, the loader operated the vehicle's radio, a task a fifth crew member performed in command Jagdpanzer IVs. The loader/radio operator used a static Rbl F 3b periscope that provided a view to starboard, but for all its vision devices, the vehicle lacked rearward visibility. Unlike the PzKpfw IV, which provided access hatches for each of its five crewmen, the Jagdpanzer IV's two hatches (commander and loader/radio operator) greatly hindered rapid exit from a burning vehicle.

Here, Waffen-SS personnel man a 7.5cm PaK 40 anti-tank gun. Although exposing its crew, this towed weapon presented a small profile and could fire high-velocity rounds from stable, semi-fixed positions. With only enough Jagdpanzer IVs to outfit two companies of the division's SS-Panzerjäger-Abteilung 12, 3./SS-PzJgAbt 12 manned PaK 40 anti-tank guns towed by 'Maultier' ('Mule') half-tracks. (Photo by Keystone-France/Gamma-Keystone via Getty Images)

Panzerjäger-Lehr-Abteilung 130 crews had conducted individual practice on their new mounts, but not as groups, while additional training with mixed formations was not considered necessary. Bayerlein emphasized gunnery exercises and marksmanship training, as well as dismounting drills. While in Hungary the battalion conducted gunnery training at the Gran and Veszprém ranges against static and moving targets, while Panzer-Aufklärungs-Lehr-Abteilung 130 and *Panzergrenadiere* practised integrating with armour or other units. Coordinated, concentrated firepower training was stressed, as were active and passive (e.g. camouflage, dispersion and concealed protected positions) air-defence and anti-tank measures. When selecting positions, Bayerlein stressed the need to safeguard the AFVs, especially against enemy anti-tank assets. Lack of a suitable training area, spare parts, medical personnel and ammunition hindered training, as did unreliable supply lorries.

Alongside the Heer, the premiere Waffen-SS formations had long demonstrated their effectiveness on the battlefield, and the untested teenagers of 12. SS-Panzer-Division *Hitlerjugend* would prove no exception. The transition to actual service was facilitated by the fact that many of *Hitlerjugend's* recruits had received pre-military training in the Hitler Youth. With limited time available in which to produce combat-ready soldiers at the Beverlo facility, lengthy classroom instruction in ballistics and other firearms theory were eliminated, as was traditional firing-range instruction and practice, in favour of training that better reflected combat. Shooting at hidden and moving targets with a variety of small arms was stressed, as was calm fire discipline amid a chaotic environment. Under a *Gruppenführer* firing instructor, progressive stations instilled a methodical execution of controlled aiming, kneeling and prone firing at 70m, 100m and 150m. Dressing-down of recruits was to be avoided in favour of corrections in measured, patient tones used to gain the recruit's trust and instill the instructor's professional, disciplined attitude. To foster camaraderie, officers were not addressed using 'Herr' before their rank, as was obligatory in other services. Towards the end of training a *Zugführer* was brought in, as live ammunition was introduced. Experience on the Eastern Front promoted proficiency in twilight and night operations that included using 'straw men', wire alarms and the like to keep the recruits alert and perceptive. Close combat was also stressed, as was shooting at low-flying aircraft.

Until their Jagdpanzer IVs arrived, SS-Panzerjäger-Abteilung 12 practised on a pair of Marder III tank destroyers. Once the assigned *Panzerjäger* vehicles became available, much of the training was similar to that of the Panzer-Lehr-Division. Over the course of just 18 weeks, *Hitlerjugend* recruits endured an often brutal regimen that served to acclimate the teenagers to the rigours of front-line duty, while political indoctrination, teamwork and comradeship forged a determined, motivated formation.

BRITISH AND POLISH TACTICS

General Montgomery sought to avoid squandering Britain's limited manpower pool to best engage and defeat the Germans, and focused on limited-objective, set-piece operations, with a sufficiently large supply build-up to provide his soldiers with everything necessary to achieve success. With Allied armoured formations often overstrength, well supplied and reinforced, they generally possessed greater potential endurance and effectiveness than their adversaries. The British trained for a rapid advance into open terrain before the Germans could respond effectively; for those British tankers who had fought in the open North African desert, the constrained Normandy terrain came as a shock.

In the nearly four years since being ejected from Continental Europe the British Army had sought to provide training that replicated and prepared its limited manpower for combat, which translated into generally thoroughly planned, set-piece operations. During the lead-up to Normandy, however, several veteran commanders were reluctant to send their men to training schools, arguing that they promoted textbook rather than realistic tactics and battlefield solutions, and that drills and strict adherence to doctrine and the chain of command stifled flexibility and initiative. Although recent lessons learned in Tunisia and Italy stressed the benefit of integrating tanks and infantry at tactical organizational levels to provide on-the-spot, mutual support, the 6pdr cannon found on the Churchill and Cromwell tanks provided limited high-explosive support effectiveness. Montgomery's promotion of developing a single, general-purpose capital tank design capable of firing both armour-piercing and high-explosive rounds never really materialized until the post-war Centurion, but in 1943 and early 1944 the British War Office needed to use what was available and in quantity. As such the relatively heavy Churchill would continue to serve in infantry-support duties while the Cromwell, with its comparatively modest armour protection and limited main armament, was typically assigned to reconnaissance duties. In 7th Armoured Division, however, the Cromwell was allocated to the offensive vanguard.

A captured, still functional Sherman Firefly named 'Alla Keefek' from A Squadron, 4th CLY east of Villers-Bocage in June 1944. Having recently engaged Tiger Is from schwere SS-Panzer-Abteilung 101, the nearby Cromwell VI and IV were similarly abandoned. Although the Sherman Firefly was 20cm higher than the Cromwell and less able to manoeuvre unseen, the former's high-velocity QF 17-pdr cannon could at least effectively engage heavier German Panthers and Tiger Is at comparable distances. The lengthy gun's overhang proved a hindrance in rough, constricted terrain, and its considerable muzzle flash could expose the Firefly's firing position or set nearby foliage alight. To accommodate the weapon's larger breech, the co-driver position was eliminated to make room for its ammunition, and the subsequently cramped fighting compartment reduced the Firefly's rate of fire. In combat the Firefly typically provided overwatch, often in hull-down positions, for friendly armour and infantry. With a deserved reputation as a tank-killer, the Firefly was made a priority target by the Germans. In an effort to mask its nature and avoid undue enemy attention, Firefly crews would often paint the barrel to look like the much shorter 75mm cannon. (Bundesarchiv Bild 101I-738-0275-02 Foto: Grimm, Arthur)

The British Cromwell tank represented an improvement over previous domestically produced designs, with excellent forward speed and mobility relative to its contemporaries. Given that the British underestimated the amount of enemy armour they would face around Caen, the vehicle seemed well-suited to conducting reconnaissance and deep-penetration duties. During the close, largely *bocage* fighting south of Tilly-sur-Seulles crews found the Cromwell to be mechanically less reliable than the M4; it was also under-armoured, and slow in reverse – an important consideration should the vehicle need to withdraw while keeping its thicker frontal armour facing the enemy. On the day 4th CLY encountered schwere SS-Panzer-Abteilung 101's Tiger Is at Villers-Bocage (13 June 1944), these Cromwells from 22nd Armoured Brigade Workshop undergo maintenance and repair. Note the nearest vehicle has 'Hessian Tape' at the ready to mask and break up the vehicle's shape with camouflage netting, and the captured MG 34 machine gun near the cupola. (© IWM B 9095)

With the British War Office continuing to field armour in two, largely separate roles as neither tank design was considered suitable to undertake the other's primary duties, while functioning within a rather disjointed armoured and infantry brigade organizational framework, pre-Normandy doctrine stressed using infantry tanks to lead an attack. Infantry followed up to help hold and secure captured ground or provide support, and cruiser tanks were to advance in a third wave to exploit opportunities. In more open terrain troops would typically advance with three Cromwells abreast, squadrons adopting a wedge formation with the squadron commander centrally located. When operating in *bocage* terrain individual tanks or troops would advance via leapfrogging, with one portion providing static support for the rest to move before exchanging roles.

During the British advance from the low, relatively open coastal terrain around Bayeux and into the fragmented *bocage* farmland, wooded areas and reinforced farms and villages to the south, they increasingly faced a dilemma. While the area's numerous unpaved roads and trails seemingly offered the best option to maintain momentum, the close surrounding terrain funnelled vehicle movement, made them vulnerable to mines, and concealed German towed anti-tank guns and *Panzerfaust/Panzerschreck*-armed tank-hunter teams. Early on, British and Canadian tanks would often advance ahead of supporting infantry; the Germans would let the armour pass, then engage the infantry before turning their attention back to the now unsupported enemy AFVs. While attacking cross-country offered tactical flexibility, it also required a time-consuming breaching of very entrenched hedgerows and operating in the intervening open areas in which Allied tanks could be engaged from a distance by hidden German armour. As it soon became evident that British armour was ill-suited to attack in such terrain, without the eyes and ears of accompanying infantry, such integration was increasingly conducted, which generally meant the foot-soldiers were increasingly sent forward to clear resistance, while the tanks provided overwatch.

Tanks could call on artillery or, if a friendly observation aircraft were about, tactical air support could be called in. To reduce the bluish exhaust smoke the Cromwell's petrol engines produced, tank commanders often ensured a fuel mix was used that

CROMWELL COMMANDERS

JOHN CLOUDSLEY-THOMPSON

Born in Murree, India on 23 May 1921, John L. Cloudsley-Thompson was a member of the Officers' Training Corps at Marlborough and Pembroke College in Cambridge early in the war. He soon volunteered with The Royal Tank Regiment, and following training at Tidworth in Wiltshire and the Royal Military College, Sandhurst in Berkshire in 1940, was commissioned into 4th Queen's Own Hussars. Transferring to 4th CLY, he was transported to its parent formation, 7th Armoured Division, serving in North Africa. Cloudsley-Thompson subsequently fought across Egypt and Libya during Operation *Crusader* in November 1941. While he served as a Crusader VI commander in June 1942, a high-explosive round struck his vehicle, killing or wounding the crew. Suffering from a severe leg injury, he spent time in hospital in Cairo and recuperated in England, where he worked as a gunnery instructor at Sandhurst.

Restless from inaction, he arranged a health upgrade to enable him to return to duty and participate in the Normandy invasion. During 7th Armoured Division's flanking movement through Villers-Bocage on 13 June 1944, Lt Cloudsley-Thompson's Cromwell (RHQ Troop, 4th CLY) was one of several victims of SS-Obersturmführer Michael Wittmann's Tiger I (2./sSS-PzAbt 101) running roughshod through the village. In July Cloudsley-Thompson participated in arguably Britain's largest tank battle, Operation *Goodwood*, which resulted in the Allies finally capturing Caen. After the war he completed his education and went on to become a zoology lecturer at King's College, London, and later a naturalist in Saharan Africa. He died on 4 October 2013.

JAN MACIEJOWSKI

Jan Maciejowski was born in Kałusz in Austria-Hungary-occupied Poland on 12 June 1904. Prior to Poland's partial mobilization on 24 March 1939, he led 11th Cavalry Squadron *Mizocz* before being hospitalized for most of August. Returning to active duty on 31 August 1939, he served with the unit throughout most of the Polish campaign. With the parent 1st Cavalry Regiment of the Border Defence Corps having been worn down during the fighting, and the squadron's commander wounded, Captain of Cavalry Maciejowski assumed the role on 26 September, only to dissolve the unit two days later to effect an escape across the border before Poland's imminent surrender. For his actions he was awarded Poland's highest military decoration, the Řád Virtuti Militari (Order of Military Virtue), Class V.

During the French campaign in 1940 he commanded 10th Mounted Rifle Regiment's Heavy Machine Gun Squadron, and in February 1942, Major Maciejowski served as 2IC 10th Mounted Rifle Regiment, with its Valentine Is and IIIs. On 8 November 1943 he was appointed the unit's commander, and soon after the regiment was allocated Cromwell tanks. 10th Mounted Rifle Regiment landed on Gold Beach on 31 July 1944, and soon went into action during Operation *Totalize* as Polish 1st Armoured Division's reconnaissance element. With Maciejowski's Cromwells leading the Polish advance on La Croix and Soignolles on 9 August, determined German resistance delayed Allied efforts and claimed numerous tanks during their push for the Falaise area. On 20 August, during the final stages of the follow-up Operation *Tractable*, Maciejowski was killed near Chambois, as his unit helped seal the 'Falaise Gap'. He was buried nearby with the posthumous rank of lieutenant-colonel.

would reduce it when in positions potentially visible to the enemy. Commanders generally slowed down when approaching a firing position to minimize the throwing up of dust that would indicate the movement. When approaching a potentially enemy-occupied village or defensive location, British tankers would normally fire their cannons and machine guns at every potential enemy position before sending in infantry to conduct a systematic search of the area, after which the tanks would advance 'brass up', firing at targets.

GERMAN TACTICS

During the Normandy campaign, proven Panzer tactics based on concentration and manoeuvre proved to be generally ill-suited to the constricted *bocage* terrain. In such an environment, units deploying the low-profile Jagdpanzer IVs acted as 'fire brigades'; their AFVs presented a difficult target, especially when firing and relocating among concealed ambush positions, preferably from an enemy's flanks or rear, and reverse slopes so that only the main gun was visible. As many stretches of road between Bayeux and Caen could be effectively contested with a well-placed tank or anti-tank gun, individual Jagdpanzer IVs commonly acted as the hub of localized *Panzergrenadier* resistance. The vehicles were typically kept hidden and uncommitted until the enemy's main point of attack was determined, and then only fired when halted.

Immobilized vehicles were to avoid engaging the enemy given the loss of mobility, and if threatened with capture or unable to be towed were instead to be blown up. The Jagdpanzer IV's machine guns were the preferred anti-personnel option at all engagement ranges rather than the main gun's high-explosive rounds to conserve ammunition for more appropriate targets, such as towed guns and built-up positions. When operating in groups, Jagdpanzer IVs fought using conventional fire-and-movement tactics where one vehicle would stop to provide support for another, as it advanced ahead to repeat the leapfrogging. During company-strength operations, one

Although towed anti-tank weapons provided a degree of crew and component protection from small-arms fire, shrapnel and muzzle blast, their low profile and high-velocity rounds could wreak havoc on armoured vehicles having to advance along the Normandy region's many constricted trails and roads. Towed weapons were much cheaper to manufacture than armoured vehicles; the cost-to-benefit ratio often worked in their favour, especially during relatively static actions. As these weapons could fire high-explosive as well as armour-piercing rounds, they could further provide a degree of artillery support, and target soft-skinned vehicles, infantry, and built-up positions. With many *Panzerjäger* battalions lacking sufficient Jagdpanzer IVs, one company often comprised towed anti-tank guns, such as this knocked-out 7.5cm PaK 40 at Fonteney-le-Pesnel, just east of Tilly-sur-Seulles, on 25 June 1944. A Panther Ausf A and a Sherman II (both immobilized) are in the near-distance. (© IWM B 5939)

JAGDPANZER IV COMMANDERS

JOACHIM BARTH

Born in Meissen, Germany on 20 April 1913, Joachim Barth was promoted to *Leutnant* on 1 April 1936, and served in the Polish and French campaigns as an adjutant in Panzerabwehr-Abteilung 13 under 13. Infanterie-Division (mot.). Reconfigured as a Panzer division for Operation *Barbarossa*, the formation fought under Heeresgruppe Süd; Oberleutnant Barth won the German Cross in Gold on 19 December 1941 for repeated acts of bravery, having already been awarded the Iron Cross 1st and 2nd classes. With Panzerjäger-Abteilung 13 (Marder IIIs) having been created on 31 January 1942, Hauptmann Barth commanded 1./PzJgAbt 13 during the advance into the Caucasus in late summer 1942. During the fighting around the Maikop oilfields and the River Terek, in which his unit helped destroy several dozen Soviet tanks, he earned the Knight's Cross on 17 December 1942. Following the Stalingrad debacle, 13. Panzer-Division fought its way into the Kuban Peninsula before relocating to the Crimea, and back through the Ukraine.

With the Panzer-Lehr-Division forming in early 1944, Major Barth was transferred to lead its Panzerjäger-Lehr-Abteilung 130, which helped counter 7th Armoured Division's push on Tilly-sur-Seulles on 10 and 11 June 1944. The formation was soon repositioned to contest the American break-out around Saint-Lô and later during the Ardennes campaign before the weakened division was surrounded in the Ruhr Pocket in April 1945 and forced to surrender. Joining the post-war Bundeswehr in 1956, Barth headed the Heeresunteroffizierschule II (Army NCO School II) in Aachen, before retiring as an *Oberst* in 1971. He died on 1 February 2002.

GEORG HURDELBRINK

Born on 6 October 1919, Georg Hurdelbrink was a member of the *Hitlerjugend* (Hitler Youth) from May 1933 until November 1936 when he joined the SS and volunteered with SS-Totenkopfverbande *Ostfriesland*, having passed the height (1.8m), age (17–22), health and racial requirements. He went on to serve with SS-Division *Totenkopf* and *Leibstandarte SS Adolf Hitler* (mot.) following the fighting in Poland and France, respectively. In November 1941, Hurdelbrink attended a two-month officer candidate stint at SS-Junkerschule Bad Tölz before being posted to *Leibstandarte's* SS-Panzerjäger-Abteilung 1 (Marder IIIs) in early 1942.

On 9 November 1943 he transferred to 12. SS-Panzer-Division *Hitlerjugend* as commander of 1./SS-PzJgAbt 12, with the rank of *SS-Obersturmführer*. During *Hitlerjugend's* efforts to prevent Polish and Canadian forces from rapidly pushing south during Operation *Totalize* on 8 August, Hurdelbrink's Jagdpanzer IVs participated in a counter-attack in the Saint-Aignan-de-Cramesnil and Garcelles-Secqueville sectors where they knocked out several Allied tanks. Over the next week the unit provided valuable support for the active German defence. With 1./SS-PzJgAbt 12 credited with destroying 86 enemy vehicles over this period, *Hitlerjugend's* commander recommended Hurdelbrink for the Knight's Cross, which was awarded two months later. Under Hurdelbrink's leadership the unit subsequently fought during the Ardennes campaign and in March 1945 against the advancing Red Army in Hungary. He died on 26 August 2002.

platoon typically provided fire support. As part of friendly withdrawals the vehicles took up positions at the rear to provide overwatch, while maintaining radio silence for security.

The Jagdpanzer IV's high-velocity 7.5cm cannon allowed it to fight at ranges beyond what was effective for many Allied armoured vehicles available in Normandy, which reciprocally minimized the disadvantages of its limited traverse, while its comparatively thick frontal plate and low profile aided survivability. On encountering anti-tank guns while on the move, Jagdpanzer IVs were to remain active and aggressively attack with all cannon firing. Supporting Jagdpanzer IVs often kept a high-explosive round in the breech in order to get a snap-shot off at anti-tank guns, as a hit nearby could still knock out the enemy crew. The limited availability of personnel meant German tank crews could be expected to remain in their cramped vehicles for several days at a stretch, unlike their adversaries, who were regularly rotated between the front line and rear areas. All tank crews, however, were subjected to a variety of physical and psychological stresses due to noise, vibration, fumes and other factors, and their combat effectiveness could become considerably degraded. Related health problems ranged from poor circulation and manual dexterity to numbness and cramping, while temperatures above 35 degrees Celsius hampered perceptual and cognitive functions, and promoted dehydration. Crews from both sides commonly dug trenches under or near their mounts to provide relatively safe areas; these could also be used for a tactical command post or makeshift medical area.

In order to maintain combat effectiveness it was essential to maintain a steady supply and efficient distribution of ammunition, fuel, lubricants, spare parts, food, medicine and a host of other necessities to the front line. While the Allies possessed overwhelming volumes of resources and *matériel*, and naval and air support allowed them to provide these services largely free from interference, the Germans – who were reliant upon road and rail transport, often from hundreds of kilometres away – found their arrangements were severely disrupted by Allied air power. During combat inconsistent supply meant German forces needed to be mindful of unnecessary expenditures, which risked degrading tactical performance and operational endurance.

Having been allocated 21 Jagdpanzer IVs on 10 July 1944, 116. Panzer-Division was soon sent to the area south-east of Caen, before being redirected westwards to sever American spearheads streaming from their 25 July break-out around Saint-Lô. In an effort to provide camouflage against aerial observation this vehicle from Panzerjäger-Abteilung 228 has affixed a liberal covering of fresh foliage. With the Allies having control over the Normandy skies, German ground forces were continuously on the alert. In addition to heavy aircraft carpet-bombing large areas into oblivion, and relatively low-flying tactical bombers that struck German airfields, road and rail networks and marshalling yards to disrupt logistics, perhaps the greatest threat was from ground-attack aircraft. British Typhoons and American P-47 Thunderbolts could provide a considerable amount of machine-gun fire and commonly carried unguided rockets that could easily penetrate the relatively thin top armour of German armoured vehicles. During Germany's ill-conceived Operation *Lüttich* (7–13 August) and in the subsequent fighting inside the Falaise Pocket the armour of 116. Panzer-Division, and other critically important German assets, was frequently halted and forced to seek cover, which hindered movement and combat operations during daytime. (Bundesarchiv Bild 101I-496-3464-05 Foto: Burchhaus)

THE STRATEGIC SITUATION

10 JUNE 1944

Second (British) Army having failed to capture Caen, on 7 June Operation *Perch* was enacted, which shifted the focus to having Lt-Gen Gerard C. Bucknall's XXX Corps penetrate into the still largely undefended area west of the city. At 1100hrs on 7 June, 56th (Independent) Infantry Brigade captured Bayeux. Having lost a handful of Cromwells to the English Channel during their landing on D+1, the three armoured regiments of 22nd Armoured Brigade (1st RTR, 5th RTR and 4th CLY) drove 20km to the Bayeux area. German snipers, often strapped to high tree branches, inflicted numerous casualties among Cromwell commanders who lacked suitable cupola protection, and chose to wear berets instead of helmets so as to use headsets more easily.

With Generalleutnant Bayerlein's command having passed through Argentan at 0200hrs on 7 June and Flers two hours later, 80km still separated it from its destination. Until it arrived 12. SS-Panzer-Division *Hitlerjugend* struggled to check two Allied infantry divisions, and the newly arriving British 7th Armoured Division. Although 21. Panzer-Division and *Hitlerjugend* had been ordered to counter-attack at midday on 6 June, the effects of aerial bombing the previous day meant that I. SS-Panzerkorps' headquarters near Thury-Harcourt lacked long-distance communications until 1440hrs on 7 June, when intermittent radio contact with Heeresgruppe B was re-established. By the afternoon, Generalfeldmarschall Erwin Rommel, responsible for defence of the French coast against an Allied invasion, had failed in his effort to eliminate I Corps due to the activity of Allied fighter-bombers and conflicting Axis orders that paralysed effective communications. While the Panzer-Lehr-Division approached to within 40km of Villers-Bocage, at 1600hrs Bayerlein finally found the headquarters of Obergruppenführer und General der Waffen-SS Josef 'Sepp' Dietrich's I. SS-Panzerkorps to receive the latest battlefield intelligence and corresponding orders to cover I. SS-Panzerkorps' exposed left flank. With *Hitlerjugend* reporting that Bayeux and the Panzer-Lehr-Division's destination zone were occupied by the enemy, Bayerlein was instructed to redirect his advance further to the west.

At 0430hrs on 8 June the Panzer-Lehr-Division's vanguard, II./PzGrenLeRgt 902 and the regimental staff, approached their revised, more westerly march objective. By 0900hrs the bulk of the Panzer-Lehr-Division began arriving along the Bayeux–Caen railway's southern edge. With Panzer-Aufklärungs-Lehr-Abteilung 130 having fanned out to conduct flank reconnaissance, Panzerjäger-Lehr-Abteilung 130 and Panzer-Lehr-Regiment 130 had yet to arrive. The Panzer-Lehr-Division's Panthers due from I./PzRgt 6 remained in transit, and were not expected for two more days. On making contact with British forces as per Dietrich's order the Panzer-Lehr-Division was to capture the Norrey-en-Bessin area and push to the coastal area around Courseulles-sur-Mer. With 21. Panzer-Division fixed astride the River Orne, and the neighbouring *Hitlerjugend* unable to gain ground against the British and Canadians, Bayerlein's lead elements began infiltrating towards Bayeux.

Although 50th Division's progress appeared in jeopardy due to an increase in localized German resistance, a break-out to the south still seemed possible using 7th Armoured Division. At 1905hrs Rommel arrived at the Panzer-Lehr-Division's headquarters; to counter the advancing British Bayerlein was ordered to regroup further west near Tilly-sur-Seulles, with the intent of recapturing Bayeux on 9 June. Once in place, I. SS-Panzerkorps would finally be able to launch a concentrated counter-attack to split and eliminate the British beachhead.

Intent on recapturing Bayeux and the surrounding area and hindering further Allied progress inland, during the morning of 9 June one of the Panzer-Lehr-Division's two *Kampfgruppen* (battlegroups) set off along the main connecting road north from Tilly-sur-Seulles. A mixed force comprising Panzergrenadier-Lehr-Regiment 901 and Panzerjäger-Lehr-Abteilung 130 proceeded along both banks of the River Seulles on Bayerlein's right. 2./PzJgLeAbt 130's six Jagdpanzer IVs remained in the rear test-firing their main guns, having recently corrected improperly aligned gunsights. After an advance of some 4km, at 1700hrs Kampfgruppe *Schönberg* captured Ellon, about halfway to Bayeux, without encountering resistance on the ground or from the air due to poor weather. While Panzer-Aufklärungs-Lehr-Abteilung 130's half-tracks, armoured cars and motorcycles pushed ahead to secure Arganchy near the Bayeux–Saint-Lô road, German elements further back reported unidentified enemy tanks heading in the opposite direction towards Tilly-sur-Seulles.

With Hitler and OKW having issued a warning that the Allies were expected to conduct their primary amphibious invasion in Belgium the next day, and *Hitlerjugend* and 21. Panzer-Division struggling to hold their ground, Dietrich ordered lead Panzer-Lehr-Division elements back to help counter the two materializing British attacks on Tilly-sur-Seulles. With I. SS-Panzerkorps having failed to organize a

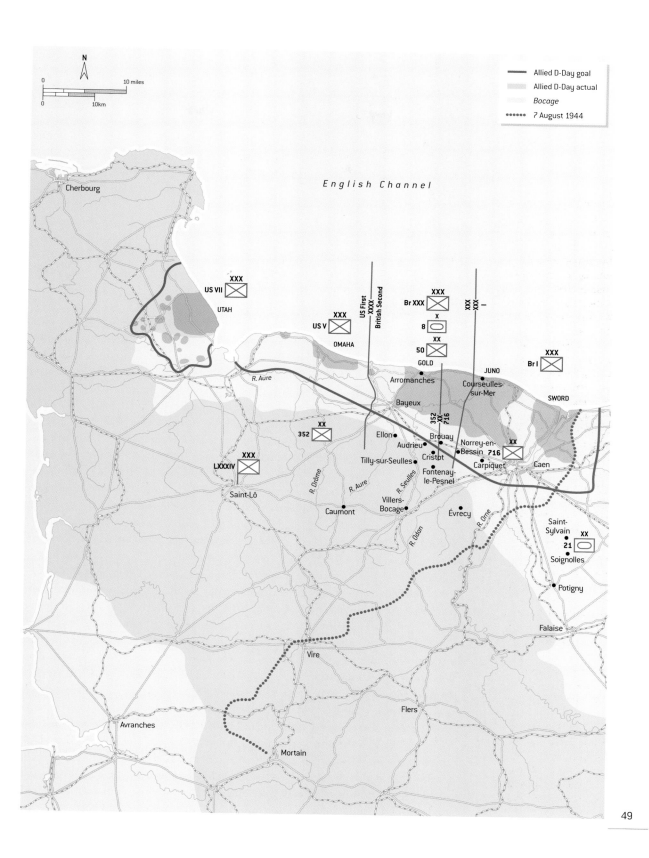

N

0   10 miles
0   10km

English Channel

Allied D-Day goal
Allied D-Day actual
Bocage
••••• 7 August 1944

Cherbourg

US VII **XXX**

UTAH

US V **XXX**

OMAHA

US First
XXXX
British Second

Br XXX **XXX**

X
8

XX
50

GOLD

XXX Br I

JUNO

Courseulles-
sur-Mer

SWORD

R. Aure

Arromanches

Bayeux

352
XX
716

352 **XX**

Ellon

Brouay

Norrey-en-
Bessin

XX 716

LXXXIV **XXX**

Audrieu

Cristot

Carpiquet

Caen

Tilly-sur-Seulles

Fontenay-
le-Pesnel

R. Drôme

R. Aure

R. Seulles

Saint-Lô

Villers-
Bocage

Évrecy

Caumont

R. Odon

R. Orne

Saint-
Sylvain

XX
21

Soignolles

Potigny

Falaise

Vire

Flers

Avranches

Mortain

49

concerted counter-attack against the Allied landings, and unable to reinforce and resupply its forces sufficiently, the Germans were increasingly forced onto the operational defensive. With the Panzer-Lehr-Division, including Panzerjäger-Lehr-Abteilung 130, having established defensive positions centred on Tilly-sur-Seulles 5km to the north-west during the night of 9/10 June, 22nd Armoured Brigade prepared to commence its push for Villers-Bocage a few hours off.

Having landed at Gold Beach on 7 June 1944, along with the rest of 4th CLY, this knocked-out Cromwell IV (T 121766 W) (also shown on page 52) remains in a wooded area just east of Villers-Bocage on 1 July, some two weeks after the fighting. As part of 22nd Armoured Brigade's spearhead A Squadron had recently halted atop Hill 213, believing the area to be lightly held at best by Panzer-Lehr-Division elements. While SS-Obersturmführer Michael Wittmann set off westward towards Villers-Bocage his 2./sSS-PzAbt 101 and later 1./sSS-PzAbt 101, and infantry from Panzergrenadier-Lehr-Regiment 901, surrounded and destroyed several British armoured vehicles in the elevated terrain, including 11 Cromwells and three Sherman Fireflies. (Keystone-France/Gamma-Keystone via Getty Images)

7 AUGUST 1944

During six weeks of largely positional warfare the Americans captured Cherbourg and steadily pushed southwards upwards of 35km from their landing beaches. On 20 July 1944 British and Canadian forces at last succeeded in capturing Caen during Operation *Goodwood*, and five days later the American break-out near Saint-Lô (Operation *Cobra*) finally ruptured the increasingly thin German defences. With First (US) Army pouring southwards, and a follow-up British effort, Operation *Bluecoat* (30 July–7 August), pushing south-west of Caen, the German position in Normandy seemed untenable. With the Westheer scrambling to counter the American break-out in the western lodgement, I. SS-Panzerkorps continued to resist British and Canadian forces south of Caen and along the Verrières Ridge. As Panzer formations were increasingly stripped from the eastern sector and sent west, General Bernard L. Montgomery, commander of Allied ground forces for Operation *Overlord*, worked towards a renewed offensive to break through the German defence on an operational scale.

Tasked with the undertaking, Lt-Gen Henry D.G. 'Harry' Crerar's Canadian First Army comprised I Corps on the extreme left and II Canadian Corps south of Caen. As part of the latter, Polish 1st Armoured Division's 10th Mounted Rifle Regiment landed at Courseulles-sur-Mer on 31 July, during which several vehicles received minor damage and one of 3rd Squadron's Cromwells was lost. Between 29 July and 4 August the unit's parent formation followed suit. In line with British practice, Brig Stanislaw Maczek's division included an armoured brigade (10th Armoured Cavalry Brigade) and an infantry brigade (3rd Infantry Brigade). During a meeting with his two superiors on 1 August, Maczek lobbied for a sufficiently broad attack zone to provide optimal tactical flexibility for his armoured division – in contrast with the narrower sectors and more controlled command structure favoured by the Poles' British and Canadian peers. While Lt-Gen Guy Simonds, II Canadian Corps' capable but uninspiring commander, felt such accommodations were acceptable, he had little regard for his subordinate officer's insight, in spite of Maczek's considerable armoured combat experience, and first-hand knowledge of German tactical methods.

Lacking an effective logistics system across France due to sustained Allied bombing, by early August the disintegrating German defenders had missed their opportunity to fall back in good order to establish new positions along the River Seine. Generalfeldmarschall Günther von Kluge, Oberbefehlshaber West, warned Hitler that the German left flank had collapsed and that it was a matter of either 'holding at Caen and abandoning western France, or dividing German forces between two battles, and risking collapse in both'. Having recently survived his most recent assassination attempt, Hitler exerted even greater direct control over operations and ordered Kluge to divide his forces. Unrealistically, the Germans would continue to hold Second (British) Army around Caen, while armoured forces were diverted to cut off American spearheads pushing rapidly along the Atlantic coast to Avranches, then west into Brittany, and more importantly to the south-east and into the German operational rear.

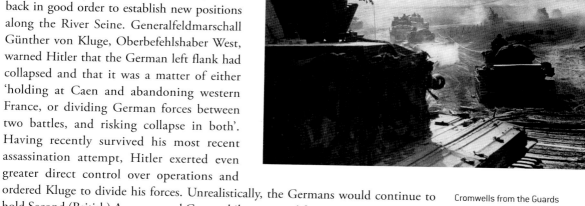

With German Panzer divisions around Caen having been replaced with infantry divisions, *Hitlerjugend* would be hard-pressed to contain the coming enemy offensive. As 2./SS-PzJgAbt 12 was declared combat-ready on 30 July it left for the battle zone between 1 and 2 August, along with the battalion staff and supply elements. Having reached its designated area within II./SS-PzGrenRgt 25's positions late on the 4th, due to an encroaching front line the consolidating SS-Panzerjäger-Abteilung 12 was quartered in Maizières and Rouvres, while its staff went to Cauvigny. 1./SS-PzJgAbt 12 would arrive the next morning, while 3./SS-PzJgAbt 12, with its 'Maultier' ('Mule' half-track)-towed 7.5cm PaK 40 anti-tank guns, remained in Escures-sur-Favières. In anticipation of imminent enemy action the next night, SS-Obersturmführer Johann Wachter's 2./SS-PzJgAbt 12 relocated to north-east of Garcelles-Secqueville.

On 5 August Montgomery met with the Poles to explain his intentions for the coming offensive. He told them that he saw Caen as a pivot from which to turn south-east to strike 7. Armee's deep right flank. To accomplish this, the armour-supported Canadian 2nd Infantry and British 51st (Highland) Infantry divisions would spearhead the advance along the right and left sides of the Caen–Falaise road, respectively. With the front line sufficiently breached the Canadian 4th Armoured and Polish 1st Armoured divisions were to push past these formations to effect a deep breakthrough. While Montgomery's briefing may have made a good impression on some in attendance, many veteran Polish tankers had reservations, including Lt-Col Franciszek Skibiński, 2IC 10th Armoured Cavalry Brigade. As a graduate of the Polish Military Academy, he felt the plan contradicted everything he had learnt in the classroom and had experienced on the battlefields of 1939–40. Informing Maczek of his concerns, especially with respect to the exposed Polish left flank, Skibiński was told by his divisional commander that Montgomery had a broader picture of the coming fight and almost assuredly had provided for the seeming deficiency.

Cromwells from the Guards Armoured Division's 2nd Armoured Reconnaissance Battalion, Welsh Guards. As all such units in the British 21st Army Group displayed a white '45' Arm of Service number set in a half-green/half-blue square, it was also applied to the Polish 10th Mounted Rifle Regiment. The nearest vehicle sports 'Hessian Tape' on its turret, which was often used on Commonwealth armour, where its numerous embedded canvas strips helped break up the vehicle's hard angles and profile. The absence of muzzle covers in such dusty conditions, and the stationary, possibly overwatching Cromwell just off-road to the far left implies a readiness for action. (Conseil Régional de Basse-Normandie / Archives Nationales du CANADA/Wikimedia/Public Domain)

COMBAT

OPERATION *PERCH*

With the British 50th Infantry Division having helped secure Gold Beach against relatively minimal resistance on 6 June, 7th Armoured Division followed suit the next day to help expand the growing beachhead. These tanks of 4th CLY are moving inland from King sector to find a suitable location to remove their waterproofing. Within a week this lead Cromwell IV, 'Chez Celibataire' (T 121766 W) from 3 Troop, A Squadron, will be destroyed during the fighting around Villers-Bocage. A Sherman Firefly, another Cromwell and soft-skinned transports follow. Note the concertina wire that has been moved aside and what looks like a stationary Crusader III triple 20mm Oerlikon anti-aircraft vehicle near the road. (© IWM B 5251)

In an effort to eject forward elements of 8th Armoured Brigade from the Saint-Pierre area, at 0615hrs on 10 June the Germans initiated an attack. At 0630hrs Major Konrad Uthe left his I./PzGrenLeRgt 901 command post in the ruined basement of what had been the Château Fortenay to lead the battalion through trails in a nearby apple orchard before moving into the relatively open farmland to advance on Saint-Pierre. With Panzergrenadier-Lehr-Regiment 902 covering the Panzer-Lehr-Division's

To make use of ageing British tanks this Crusader III has been converted to a Mk III anti-aircraft version, which mounts twin 20mm Oerlikon guns to provide mobile anti-aircraft support. This 22nd Armoured Brigade column moving inland from Gold Beach on D+1 includes US-built Stuart V light tanks, which were commonly used for reconnaissance roles. These tanks possess wading stacks to keep seawater from entering the engines during landing and which will be removed once the vehicles are sufficiently inland. Note the barrage balloon in the distance to deter low-flying German aircraft from intervening. (© IWM B 5124)

left flank west of the River Seulles, Uthe attacked Saint-Pierre and the nearby Hill 103 at 0700hrs using infiltrating grenadiers and half-tracks that included SdKfz 251/9 *Stummel* ('stumps') equipped with short-barrelled 7.5cm guns. I./PzRgt 6 and II./PzLeRgt 130, with Panther and PzKpfw IV tanks respectively, struck north from near Fontenay-le-Pesnel against 8th Armoured Brigade. Several two- and three-man German tank-hunting teams from I./PzGrenLeRgt 901 exploited the more restricted terrain to approach and destroy five Sherman IIIs of 24th Lancers near Saint-Pierre using handheld weapons such as the *Panzerfaust* and *Panzerschreck*, as well as grenades placed under one AFV's turret and another batch dropped down an unlocked hatch.

Buckling under the pressure, elements of 8th Battalion, The Durham Light Infantry (8th DLI) suddenly withdrew to the north, weakening Saint-Pierre's defence. 288 Anti-Tank Battery's four M10 self-propelled guns and some of the unit's eight 6-pdr anti-tank-gun crews followed suit, although some of the latter continued to fight, and succeeded in immobilizing a Panther. While these towed guns could be manoeuvred within the confined *bocage* terrain relatively easily and could penetrate PzKpfw IVs and a Panther's side armour, anti-tank gunners assigned to 50th Division also fielded heavier and larger 17-pdr (76mm) equivalents. Between Saint-Pierre and Hill 103, Allied artillery, armour and air-directed naval gunfire targeted the Tilly-sur-Seulles–Juvigny-sur-Seulles–Fontenay-le-Pesnel area; with fighter-bombers attacking German reinforcements moving towards the sector, 8th Armoured Brigade was able to assume an intractable defensive posture.

THE JÉRUSALEM CROSSROADS

After a rainy night, at 0800hrs on 10 June, 56th (Independent) Infantry Brigade was placed under 7th Armoured Division's control to coordinate with armour and provide flank protection along the River Aure. War Office doctrine stressed that the armour in an armoured division and its organic infantry brigade were to be kept separate to avoid constraining the former's freedom of movement, and although feasible in predominantly open terrain in which they expected to fight, the realities of the constricted *bocage* necessitated tactical changes in the field. Along with 151st Infantry Brigade, this provided some badly needed infantry, as 7th Armoured Division's 131st Infantry Brigade had yet to land, and 22nd Armoured Brigade's organic 1st Battalion, The Rifle Brigade, which was to provide one motor company to each armoured regiment, possessed light Universal Carriers that lacked the necessary protection to advance into combat alongside tanks.

At the beginning of the day, 4th CLY was assembled at the village of Sommervieu, some 2km north-east of Bayeux. Having coordinated with 2nd Battalion, The South Wales Borderers (2nd SWB) and supporting units to eliminate German resistance at Sully on 9 June, 5th RTR occupied positions north-west of Bayeux. Until 131st Infantry Brigade arrived 1st RTR at Rucqueville would act as a reserve and help secure communications over the River Seulles bridges, while 8th King's Royal Irish Hussars, effectively 22nd Armoured Brigade's fourth armoured regiment, having just landed the previous day, would also stay out of the 10 June fighting. At 0830hrs, British forces set off from just south of Bayeux to secure Tilly-sur-Seulles before advancing towards Villers-Bocage. 5th RTR and 4th CLY spearheaded the right and left columns, respectively, and although both groups operated sufficiently close to each other to provide mutual support if needed, by 1100hrs German snipers, tank-hunting teams and strongly held roadblocks had temporarily halted both attacks after a few kilometres. The high, predominantly *bocage* farmland around Monceaux-en-Bessin that sloped down to the River Aure forced the British tanks to use the few narrow trails available and risk being ambushed at close range, or move across the more open and exposed cornfields and farmland, which made them vulnerable to fire from anti-tank guns. To further bolster their entrenched, obscured defences the Germans commonly reinforced the region's numerous vernacular-style buildings and farmhouses that appeared externally innocuous. As British Cromwell and Firefly crews grew wise to Normandy's numerous hidden threats, they tended to hold back to provide overwatch support from which to 'shoot the infantry in' to clear any immediate resistance. 7th Armoured Division's previous experience with mobile operations in North Africa's very open terrain translated poorly in the present environment, and too often tanks left their accompanying infantry behind, and exposed the weaknesses of both unit types. Having minimal training in such matters, units found that inter-unit coordination was painfully learned in the field.

With 5th RTR's B and C squadrons leading the British attack's right column, follow-on infantry support enabled the tankers to continue their advance across the relatively open country around Blary, and along the Aure's right bank. As was customary, each of a British tank squadron's four troops would daily alternate taking the lead. As each bridge was passed, 2nd SWB established a protective guard and one anti-tank gun should these crossings be needed for tactical flexibility or to protect

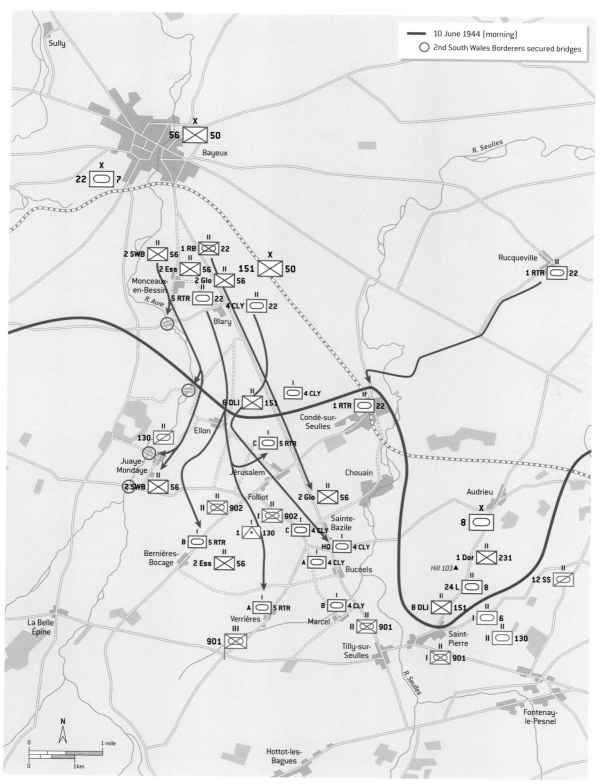

Sully

10 June 1944 (morning)
2nd South Wales Borderers secured bridges

R. Seulles

X
56 ☒ 50

Bayeux

X
22 ▭ 7

Rucqueville

II
1 RTR ▭ 22

II
2 SWB ☒ 56

II
1 RB ☒ 22

II
2 Ess ☒ 56

X
151 ☒ 50

II
2 Glo ☒ 56

Monceaux-
en-Bessin

R. Aure

II
5 RTR ▭ 22

II
4 CLY ▭ 22

Blary

I
4 CLY ▭

II
6 DLI ☒ 151

II
1 RTR ▭ 22

Condé-sur-
Seulles

II
130 ⊘

Ellon

C
5 RTR ▭

Jérusalem

Chouain

II
2 SWB ☒ 56

Juaye-
Mondaye

II
902 ☒

Folliot

II
2 Glo ☒ 56

Audrieu

X
8 ▭

I
902 ☒

Sainte-
Bazile

I
130 △

C
4 CLY ▭

II
1 Dor ☒ 231

B
5 RTR ▭

Bernières-
Bocage

II
2 Ess ☒ 56

HQ
4 CLY ▭

A
4 CLY ▭

Bucéels

Hill 103 ▲

II
24 L ▭ 8

II
12 SS ⊘

II
8 DLI ☒ 151

La Belle
Épine

A
5 RTR ▭

Verrières

B
4 CLY ▭

Marcel

I
6 ▭

II
901 ☒

Saint-
Pierre

II
130 ▭

III
901 ☒

Tilly-sur-
Seulles

R. Seulles

I
901 ☒

Fontenay-
le-Pesnel

N

0   1 mile
0   1km

Hottot-les-
Bagues

During 7th Armoured Division's advance on Tilly-sur-Seulles on 10 June, 6th DLI encountered resistance near the Jérusalem crossroads and Douet, some 500m to the north-east. During the scrap A Company, 6th DLI drove off a late-model PzKpfw IV Ausf H, and B Company, 6th DLI then knocked it out using a 6-pdr anti-tank gun. Here, 7th Armoured Division officers and a Canadian captain inspect the vehicle later in the day. (© IWM B 5375)

22nd Armoured Brigade's western flank. As A Squadron, 5th RTR and elements from 2nd Battalion, The Essex Regiment (now under 22nd Armoured Brigade) approached Ellon, a Cromwell had a track severed, apparently due to a hit by a *Panzerfaust* projectile. Other rounds similarly emanated from the cemetery of the 16th-century church of Saint-Pierre but with little effect. With German armour having been seen around Ellon B and C squadrons, 5th RTR pushed further south only to encounter resistance near the hamlet of Jérusalem from elements of I./PzGrenLeRgt 902 and parts of Ost-Bataillon 441, the latter a German-led unit of captured Russian and Belorussian soldiers that was tactically subordinated to 716. Infanterie-Division. These *Hilfswilliger* ('willing helpers') had chosen such service to fight Stalin or simply to avoid prisoner-of-war camps, and performed roles such as security, fortification construction and logistics, although they commonly dissolved or surrendered during combat.

As the tank-heavy 22nd Armoured Brigade struggled to overcome elements of I./PzGrenLeRgt 902 around Jérusalem, a German shaped-charge round immobilized the track of a Stuart V light tank providing reconnaissance for 4th CLY, and 6th DLI was brought forward to help eliminate such close-range resistance. On the brigade's left, 4th CLY advanced slowly through 6th DLI just east of Ellon, with its reconnaissance elements leading. Major P.M.R. Scott's A Squadron and Captain I.B. 'Ibby' Aird's B Squadron followed on the left and right, respectively, with Major P. McColl's

C Squadron in reserve on the Bayeux–Tilly-sur-Seulles road, 7th Armoured Division's 'centre line', or main route running through its planned line of attack. While C Squadron, 5th RTR established a protective stance near the Jérusalem crossroads, a German assembly position was discovered about half a kilometre away at Folliot. Although a Cromwell from C Squadron, 5th RTR knocked out a PzKpfw IV, their forward elements had to withdraw until 2nd SWB arrived. B Squadron, 5th RTR was subsequently ordered to find a gap on the regiment's right flank, during which time friendly fire from 8th Armoured Brigade knocked out two Cromwells of A Squadron, 4th CLY immediately west of Chouain.

While advancing on the right flank towards Verrières through Blary, Ellon and Folliot, 5th RTR's B and C squadrons made slow progress along the area's constricted *bocage* roads; 5th RTR managed the day's greatest progress, having made it to Verrières. As the British advanced southwards, many French civilians emerged to offer celebratory food and wine, although some were resentful at having the war brought to their doorstep. Regardless, British orders were to keep moving, although opportunities to supplement their composite or 24-hour ration packs with fresh eggs and milk were seldom spurned.

In the late afternoon five Cromwells from B Squadron, 5th RTR suddenly appeared behind I./PzGrenLeRgt 902's forwardmost positions and advanced on a farmhouse near Jérusalem that served as the German unit's headquarters. Having received and tested his now combat-ready Jagdpanzer IVs just a few days previously, Oberleutnant Werner Wagner, acting commander of 1./PzJgLeAbt 130, found himself in an excellent position nearby from which to engage the threat. He watched as one of the Cromwells stopped, and its commander opened his hatch the better to view the situation before disappearing back down into his turret, as its main gun traversed on the structure and fired. Quickly, Wagner coordinated his tank-hunters into suitable positions from which their limited-traverse guns could be most effective. One vehicle fired at the furthest Cromwell, which after being penetrated erupted in flames. A second British tank received two immobilizing rounds in its tracks, but when it continued to fire wildly at perceived targets, a third 7.5cm Pzgr Patr 39 KwK 40 armour-piercing projectile struck it between the turret and hull, which killed the crew. According to German reports, a third Cromwell was set alight and bottomed out in a ditch, while the remaining B Squadron vehicles similarly got stuck. Amid several more impacting rounds the British tankers abandoned their shot-up mounts, and nearby German infantry fired on them with small arms, killing several and inducing the remainder to surrender. Even though maintenance personnel were usually tasked with the removal of dead, often charred comrades, armour crews of both sides were well aware of the carnage penetrating rounds inflicted.

On hearing of this unexpected engagement, Bayerlein had his staff-car driver take him from Sermentot to Wagner's location, along with the commander's liaison, Hauptmann Alexander Hartdegen. Concerned that such an action might herald a larger British armoured thrust in his sector, and with US aircraft having recently attacked the Panzer-Lehr-Division's fuel trains west of Saint-Lô, Bayerlein was stunned to see numerous 4th CLY tanks in the relatively open terrain north of Tilly-sur-Seulles. Seemingly unconcerned about being attacked, the British vehicles were organized along a narrow front to facilitate control, concentrate firepower and enable follow-on

forces to help maintain momentum. While a tired Bayerlein waited, Hartdegen was sent off to bring forward whatever forces he could quickly gather to engage the enemy.

Hartdegen soon returned with four Panthers and a couple of 8.8cm FlaK 36 towed anti-aircraft guns from Heeres-Flak-Artillerie-Abteilung 311, which immediately established firing positions without being detected. According to German reports the tanks and then the anti-tank guns opened fire into the laager's centre, with several British tanks, lorries and fuel vehicles being set alight. British crews and soldiers scrambled to vacate the area, with some Cromwells succeeding. Three British tanks charged Bayerlein's elevated position, but the anti-tank guns turned them into smouldering wrecks, although others were able to outmanoeuvre effective German targeting.

When large-calibre naval shells began landing within the German position, which spewed considerable shrapnel and churned up the earth, Bayerlein ordered a hasty withdrawal. As per Panzer-Aufklärungs-Lehr-Abteilung 130's request for additional firepower, five Panther Ausf A tanks from I./PzRgt 6 (on loan from 3. Panzer-Division) arrived at around 1600hrs at Juaye-Mondaye, having previously allocated elements to the Saint-Pierre fight. After some minor engagements, the tankers of C Squadron, 5th RTR pulled back towards Jérusalem to halt for the night.

For the time being the British found it impossible to cross the Ruisseau du Pont Saint-Esprit Creek to extend their right flank, as the Germans had mined the crossings at Marcel and the nearby Bayeux–Tilly-sur-Seulles road. At 1800hrs, 2nd Battalion, The Essex Regiment reached the monastery at Juaye-Mondaye to find it reinforced and vigorously defended, but after 90 minutes of fighting, a British infantry assault with supporting artillery fire finally silenced German resistance.

Fighting near Bernières-Bocage remained confused. At 2030hrs, 2nd SWB concentrated around Ellon, while 2nd Battalion, The Essex Regiment remained in the Folliot area. That evening 4th CLY established laagers, with A and HQ squadrons half a kilometre north of Bucéels, B Squadron immediately east of Marcel, and C Squadron north of Sainte-Bazile. At dusk, infantry established protective screens around the tanks, whose crews ate, attended to minor maintenance and managed three or four hours of sleep before a customary 0400hrs 'stand to'.

By day's end 7th Armoured and 50th Infantry divisions had managed to advance just 7km. Having failed to penetrate German defences near Tilly-sur-Seulles and consequently propagate his own offensive, Montgomery cabled the Chief of the British Imperial Staff, Sir Alan Brooke, to say he intended to draw the enemy onto Second (British) Army in order to weaken their western defence and facilitate an American break-out. With the Allies having established a promising lodgement on the continent, however, Churchill was confident of eventual victory and subsequently had the British Cabinet create a Draft Instrument of Surrender for Germany.

Stuart Vs of 8th Hussars on 15 June. Although 8th Hussars was the armoured reconnaissance regiment for 7th Armoured Division, the regiment's weather-delayed arrival at Gold Beach meant it missed participating in the 10 June advance on Tilly-sur-Seulles. (© IWM B 5608)

THE FIGHT FOR TILLY-SUR-SEULLES

On 11 June, elements of Panzergrenadier-Lehr-Regiment 901 weathered a British naval and artillery bombardment that pummelled the now desolate landscape around Tilly-sur-Seulles. When the barrage moved off to the south, British ground forces refrained from advancing, seemingly unsure as to whether the German defences had been adequately weakened. American P-47 Thunderbolts swept in, often as low as 50m, to strafe and bomb the Panzer-Lehr-Division's positions. German 8.8cm, 2cm and assorted other anti-aircraft weapons struck several of the aircraft, some of which subsequently careened into the ground to explode. Once Allied aircraft had exited the battle zone, British armour and infantry began advancing into an obliterated and seemingly unoccupied landscape. With much of Panzergrenadier-Lehr-Regiment 901 having survived, its personnel soon emerged from their dugouts and defensive positions to offer resistance. Grazing German machine-gun fire added to the enemy's uncertainty, and the British assault waned. After 30 more minutes of preparatory artillery fire, a renewed British attack moved on Tilly-sur-Seulles, but 30cm Nebelwerfer rockets from four launchers of Werfer-Brigade 7, located 2km to the German rear, caused renewed chaos. With word spreading through the German lines of the oncoming Cromwells and

CROMWELL IV GUNSIGHT

To engage a target, the Cromwell's commander estimated the range, and the gunner chose a corresponding sight mark for the main gun – at left: 500yd (457m), 1,000yd (914m), 1,500yd (1,372m) – and the coaxial machine gun – at right: 400yd (366m), 800yd (732m), 1,200yd (1,097m). The sight reticle on the No. 50×3 ML Mk II gun 'scope provided 3× magnification and a 13-degree field of view. In addition the 'ML' part of the No. 50×3 ML Mk II used a moving reticle – the horizontal bar with cross hair and lead lines moved up or down depending upon the range setting of the gunner. The gunner also used spade grips to control the turret's electric rotation, which had a mode switch for 'coarse' or 'fine' movement. On firing, the Cromwell rocked and the breech recoiled amid a painfully loud report. The ejected shell case hit the back of the canvas chute before falling into a canvas bag. British sights lacked range settings for APDS and APCR ammunition, which were in rather short supply anyway. As with the Churchill infantry tank, care needed to be taken when traversing the turret during an engagement, as certain angles blocked the driver's escape hatch.

Fireflies, Hauptmann Julius Oventrop dispatched six Jagdpanzer IVs from his 3./PzJgLeAbt 130 to the scene and had them establish positions along a reverse slope. The Cromwells advanced in a tight formation from the same area as the previous day near a local horse farm, 'Ferme Cheval Rouge', with individual tanks stopping to fire.

Directing the German fire from a forward shell crater, Leutnant Schönrath led his vehicles into a counter-attack once the initial firing concluded; his Jagdpanzer IV moved forward with Oberfeldwebel Erich Stolz's Jagdpanzer IV right behind. Stolz's gunner, Eduard Job, had previously served with Panzerjäger-Abteilung 13 (13. Panzer-Division) under Major Joachim Barth. Job sighted one Cromwell moving through a recent naval-fire crater and put a round through its frontal armour and set the vehicle alight, which detonated ready rounds that killed the crew. Stolz's driver adjusted the

JAGDPANZER IV GUNSIGHT

During an engagement the commander would typically identify targets, and pertinent information including their priority, direction, range and the ammunition type to use. Once the Jagdpanzer IV was generally oriented towards the threat the gunner looked through his 5× Sfl ZF 1a periscope while manually operating the main gun's traverse and elevation wheels to position the apex of the reticle's central triangle on the target. By comparing the target's general physical dimensions, speed and direction against the superimposed horizontal triangles (two apexes equating to four imaginary mils (*Striche*) depicting one metre at one kilometre), range and lead estimation could be further refined. For targets moving perpendicular to the

Jagdpanzer IV's cannon the following *Striche* respectively provided a lead: 3,4 (10km/h), 6,8 (20km/h) and 9,12 (30km/h) for the Pzgr 39 and Sprgr 42 at 600m. Engaging moving targets beyond 1,200m was not recommended as hitting the target was unlikely. German sights had coated optics and large objective lenses, which increased the brightness of the targeted image. The coaxial MG 42 machine gun's KZF 2 sight provided 1.8× magnification and calibration up to 1,200m. The commander, or another Jagdpanzer IV crewman, provided assistance with shot corrections, as part of a relatively unencumbered targeting system that saved a well-trained gunner valuable seconds when achieving the first aimed shot was paramount.

Jagdpanzer IV's orientation to better engage additional AFVs and Stolz announced a new target at 400m, which was also set alight.

The remaining Cromwells continued to advance on a comparatively broader front than normal, with infantry in support. As the lead Cromwells approached to within 50m of the German forward line, *Panzergrenadiere* fired *Panzerfaüste* that scored several hits. The six Jagdpanzer IVs leapfrogged ahead, with alternating AFVs halting to provide stable covering positions. The Jagdpanzer IVs pushed into the British-held territory and along with a handful of PzKpfw IV tanks from Panzer-Lehr-Regiment 130, and Panzergrenadier-Lehr-Regiment 901, the German forces compelled a British withdrawal. Taking advantage of the subsequent lull in the fighting, the Germans evacuated their wounded and rebuilt their positions.

A Cromwell IV from 4th CLY (likely Regimental Headquarters' T187577) in Normandy during a break on 17 June 1944, some four days after schwere SS-Panzer-Abteilung 101 Tiger Is roughly checked 7th Armoured Division at Villers-Bocage during the British flanking manoeuvre west of Tilly-sur-Seulles. During such stops, precious time was available for vehicle maintenance, laundry, resting and cooking. Note the bread loaves on the hull, plugs in both machine guns to keep out debris and what looks to be patching around the bow machine gun and the mantlet opening. (© IWM B 5681)

By the afternoon of 12 June, 7th Armoured Division had been withdrawn from the Tilly-sur-Seulles front and directed further westwards in preparation for a renewed flanking attack directed at Villers-Bocage. Although the initial movement went well for the British, on passing through the village the next day schwere SS-Panzer-Abteilung 101's Tiger I tanks took advantage of their fortuitous positioning to savage 4th CLY and 1st Battalion, The Rifle Brigade, effectively halting the British effort. With the Panzer-Lehr-Division having checked the enemy's effort to flank them, and 2. Panzer-Division arriving, on 15 June 50th Division and 7th Armoured Division settled into positions from near Tilly-sur-Seulles to La Belle Épine and to the south-west. The Panzer-Lehr-Division's efforts assisted in maintaining German control over Tilly-sur-Seulles, which helped the Germans retain Caen by preventing the city's envelopment from the west, resulting in Operation *Wild Oats* (the Allied plan to take Caen in a pincer movement) being postponed on 13 June, and cancelled a week later.

BREAK-OUT FROM NORMANDY

Having advanced throughout the night on 7/8 August, at 0130hrs II Canadian Corps' attack broke through the in-depth German defences at several places astride the Caen–Falaise road. The columns from Canadian 2nd Infantry Division on the offensive's

Polish tankers of 1st Squadron, 10th Mounted Rifle Regiment conduct maintenance on their Cromwell at the start of Operation *Totalize*, south of Caen, on 8 August 1944. Track links of various connections cover much of the turret and hull as added protection. On the turret, note the new-style helmet, generally dispensed with in favour of the beret. As with any weapon, however large, the Cromwell's main gun had to have propellant residue and debris cleaned out regularly to prolong the barrel's life and maintain firing accuracy. (© IWM MH 1405)

right were delayed by fog and unexpected opposition, but by midday they had finally captured Verrières Ridge. Senior staff were generally of the opinion that the Canadians and British could take on the Germans without losing cohesion or morale, but with the area having recently been subjected to preparatory carpet-bombing and heavy artillery fire the largely destroyed road network slowed and disrupted the predominantly mechanized forces' movement. Many infantrymen continued to rely on lightly armoured, open-topped half-tracks and Universal Carriers, and heavier Kangaroos (converted M7 Priests), while others simply rode on friendly tanks.

The Allies were soon poised to move against Cintheaux, some 3km south of their furthest penetration, but Lt-Gen Simonds, II Canadian Corps' commander, ordered a halt to allow field artillery and Canadian 4th and Polish 1st Armoured divisions to move into position to lead the operation's second phase. Whenever these armoured formations halted for an extended period, all tanks and vehicles were to be widely

Cromwell IVs from 1st Squadron, 10th Mounted Rifle Regiment head south along the Caen–Falaise Road, as Operation *Totalize* commenced on 8 August 1944. The relatively dense grouping of vehicles and the look of a parade-ground manoeuvre illustrate the Allies' near-complete control of the airspace over Normandy. On 9 August the Poles would enter the fight at Cramesnil where they would soon engage 1./SS-PzJgAbt 12 and other *Hitlerjugend* elements. (© IWM MH 1417)

A Cromwell from 10th Mounted Rifle Regiment awaits the call to action during Operation *Totalize*, August 1944. In line with its reconnaissance role the unit typically operated ahead of Polish 1st Armoured Division to provide timely intelligence. Unlike the lighter Stuart tank, the Cromwell could engage the enemy in a stand-up fight and proactively help shape a battle's course. Although the country south of Caen was generally open, armoured vehicles needed to remain relatively unencumbered with equipment to facilitate movement through the area's woods and hedgerows. Note that these tankers wear berets because helmets impeded the use of headsets, although there appears to be a helmet on the turret's starboard lifting hoop. (© IWM HU 99807)

OPPOSITE

With First (US) Army having operationally penetrated German lines around Saint-Lô in late July 1944, 1. SS, 9. SS and 116. Panzer-Divisionen moved from the Caen sector and headed west to seal the American breach. Seeking to exploit the situation, Montgomery initiated Operation *Totalize* in a renewed effort to secure Falaise and inflict a decisive defeat. Following Allied carpet-bombing and heavy-artillery fire between 2200hrs and 0030hrs during the night of 7/8 August to soften the German positions in depth, 12. SS-Panzer-Division *Hitlerjugend* sought to contest the Allied effort, which was to be conducted along a relatively narrow, constricted frontage. Once British and Canadian infantry had driven into the German defences, armoured formations, including the Polish 1st Armoured Division, expected to push through any remaining resistance.

dispersed and all crews were required to dig a shallow rectangular trench at least 70cm deep under their mounts to house up to half a dozen soldiers in relative safety. At 0800hrs, 10th Armoured Cavalry Brigade reached Bras, having undertaken an approach march of nearly 30km, and over the next four hours II Canadian Corps consolidated its gains in the Caillouet–Hill 122–Saint-Aignan-de-Cramesnil area. With the infantry having penetrated into the German defences at around 1000hrs, Polish 1st Armoured Division arrived at its jump-off area east of the Caen–Falaise road alongside Canadian 4th Armoured Division.

At 1300hrs elements of Kampfgruppe *Waldmuller* (SS-Panzergrenadier-Regiment 25) counter-attacked north towards Gaumesnil and Saint-Aignan-de-Cramesnil using its four Tiger Is, ten tank destroyers, 20 PzKpfw IVs and Panthers, and some 550 *Panzergrenadiere*. With the overwhelming number of Allied tanks pushing south, the Germans sought to exploit their longer-range AFV armament in the relatively open terrain to delay the advance. Between 1230hrs and 1355hrs, US Army Air Force B-17 Flying Fortresses bombed the second German position between Bretteville-sur-Laize and Saint-Sylvain. As per Mission No. 531, the US Eighth Air Force committed 681 B-17s and 100 P-51 Mustangs to bombing enemy strongpoints and concentrations south of Caen, including Cauvicourt (231 bombers), Bretteville-sur-Laize (99), Saint-Sylvain (99), Gouvix (1) and 67 targets of opportunity. During the operation, one bomber squadron peeled away from the main force and veered threateningly towards Polish ground forces, who threw yellow smoke to indicate 'friendly' forces. As that colour matched what the B-17 crews were using to mark targets, the errant lead bomber and follow-on planes dropped their payloads. In the ensuing chaos of explosions, debris, smoke and shockwaves, one Cromwell tank was thrown into the air, and Polish tankers scrambled for the recently dug shelters under their mounts, while fires detonated several nearby ammunition dumps over the next 40 minutes. With the aerial bombardment soon over, the shaken, resentful Polish tankers emerged to find at least three Cromwells overturned.

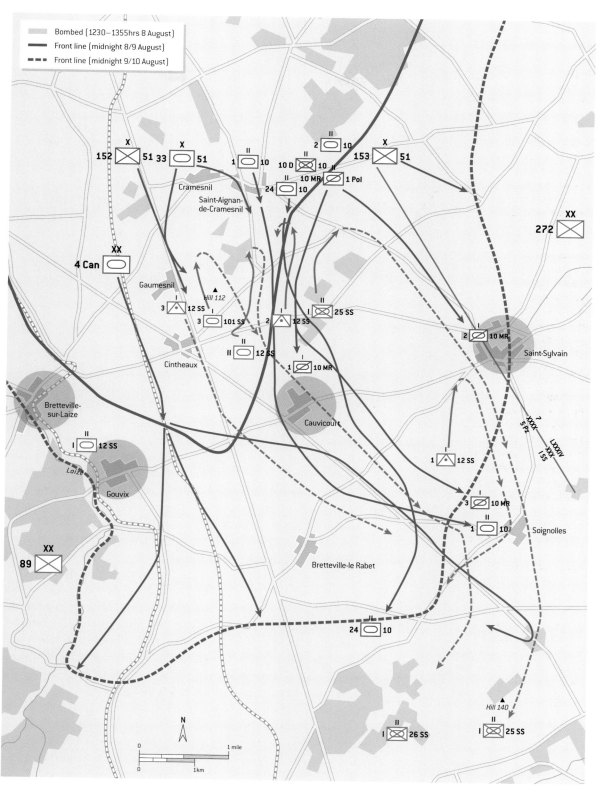

With Allied air supremacy essentially assured over the Normandy region, formations such as Polish 1st Armoured Division were able to move into assembly positions as if on parade. For the Germans, exposed areas such as this stretch of farmland between Caen and Cintheaux were generally avoided during the daytime. While Shermans, such as this Sherman V (left), equipped the formation's two armoured regiments the Cromwell was only used by 10th Mounted Rifle Regiment, which operated in the reconnaissance role. Although the Cromwell's modest armour protection and main gun meant the vehicle was ill-suited for fighting in *bocage* country, its speed and manoeuvrability proved advantageous in the largely open terrain towards Falaise. To the far left a column of soft-skinned transports similarly awaits the opportunity to advance into combat. While providing tactical infantry flexibility, lorries lacked the protection to accompany armoured vehicles directly into combat. (© IWM B 8835)

SAINT-AIGNAN-DE-CRAMESNIL

In spite of the aerial bombardment, at 1355hrs the second phase of Operation *Totalize* commenced, with Polish 1st and Canadian 4th Armoured divisions striking southwards astride the Caen–Falaise road. Unlike his Canadian peers, Maczek opted for forgoing a preparatory artillery bombardment, and instead allocated the asset as support for his advance. While 10th Armoured Cavalry Brigade was to secure Hill 140 by day's end, 3rd Infantry Brigade was to capture Cauvicourt. The *Hitlerjugend* commander, SS-Oberführer Kurt Meyer, had already ordered infantry from various German formations shattered by the bombers to join an armoured attack force to occupy Cintheaux. At 1425hrs 1./SS-PzJgAbt 12, having been combat-active since 20 June, discovered the onrushing Polish 2nd Tank and 24th Uhlan regiments just over 1km east of Saint-Aignan-de-Cramesnil. Once 10th Armoured Cavalry Brigade's leading regiments had crossed the Bretteville-le Rabet–Saint-Sylvain road, 10th Mounted Rifle Regiment, minus one squadron but reinforced with an anti-tank battery of self-propelled 17-pdrs, scouted ahead and covered the division's exposed left flank. During the ensuing combat Jagdpanzer IVs positioned around Hill 112 reportedly destroyed 16 to 18 of an estimated 22 M4 Shermans of C Squadron, 1st Northamptonshire Yeomanry for a loss of five Tiger Is, four Panthers, six PzKpfw IVs and five Jagdpanzer IVs. Two Jagdpanzer IVs from SS-Obersturmführer Hurdelbrink's 1./SS-PzJgAbt 12 advanced further through eastern Saint-Aignan-de-Cramesnil. At the village's northern edge, Hurdelbrink claimed to have knocked out

a further five tanks, an armoured reconnaissance vehicle and two prime movers. As the first wave of Polish tanks attacked southwards from Cramesnil, elements of Kampfgruppe *Waldmuller* unleashed voluminous fire that set several Shermans alight, and soon destroyed 26 of 33 tanks committed by 2nd Tank Regiment. Three Tiger Is accounted for the destruction of seven enemy tanks. 24th Uhlan Regiment correspondingly stopped its attack, and at 1450hrs Polish artillery fire was called in to provide cover.

Elements of 10th Mounted Rifle Regiment advance during Operation *Totalize* on 8 August 1944. Many crews eschewed their helmets, as berets were more accommodating for their headsets. (© IWM B 8831)

The Tiger Is and PzKpfw IVs attacking to 1./SS-PzJgAbt 12's left were unable to enter Saint-Aignan-de-Cramesnil during the day due to heavy Allied resistance. This correspondingly brought the Jagdpanzer IVs under heavy flanking fire from enemy anti-tank guns and infantry weapons. Allied tanks were also in the village, with one knocking out a Jagdpanzer IV from 1./SS-PzJgAbt 12; elements of I./SS-PzGrenRgt 25 were finally able to pull their vehicles and wounded from the sector and withdraw to Soignolles. Elements of 24th Uhlan Regiment were subjected to heavy German artillery fire, and Lt-Col Skibiński requested artillery fire on the discovered targets.

At 1520hrs the Poles established contact with Canadian 4th Armoured Division, some 2km north-west of Cintheaux. By day's end, 10th Armoured Cavalry Brigade had damaged or destroyed one PzKpfw IV, five Panthers and two 8.8cm anti-tank guns. Although the terrain was largely open, the numerous woods and hedges provided sufficient cover for German armour to operate, making attacking difficult. Angry at the lack of progress, at 2100hrs Simonds ordered an improved coordination of the

A column of Cromwell IVs from Troop 'Barbara', 1st Squadron, 10th Mounted Rifle Regiment near Saint-Aignan-de-Cramesnil on 8 August 1944. The white Arm of Service '45' within a half-green/half-blue square indicated a cruiser tank assigned to a British/Commonwealth armoured reconnaissance regiment. (National Digital Archive, Poland/CC0 1.0)

advance through the night to be executed by two infiltrating armoured battlegroups.

In the developing fight, nine Cromwells from 10th Mounted Rifle Regiment manoeuvred around I./SS-PzGrenRgt 25 on the Maizières Estrées-la-Campagne highway, which severed the German battalion's logistics. SS-Oberscharführer Rudolf Roy's gunner, SS-Rottenführer Fritz Eckstein, reportedly destroyed all of these vehicles in a short time around Hill 111, with Hurdelbrink's vehicle knocking out six more. During the day, heavy artillery, mortar and infantry fire on I./SS-PzGrenRgt 25 forced its withdrawal at 2200hrs; 1./SS-PzJgAbt 12 had already begun to do so 30 minutes earlier. During the German disengagement, Shermans from the Polish 1st Armoured Regiment suddenly attacked Soignolles. Hurdelbrink's and Roy's Jagdpanzer IVs secured the village's outskirts and struck the Polish armour in the flank. Soon 1./SS-PzJgAbt 12 had eliminated an estimated 22 Shermans and Cromwells. With the Polish attackers subsequently lacking the desire to continue the fight, the Germans were able to disengage from the area. 1./SS-PzJgAbt 12 remained attached to Kampfgruppe *Waldmuller* for defending the hills north of Maizières to Hill 140. Acting as a rearguard, at 2230hrs 1./SS-PzJgAbt 12 left Soignolles and reached Maizières later that night.

Although the Canadian and Polish offensive continued the next day to a depth of 5km, Simonds was furious with II Canadian Corps' slow progress. Maczek attempted to explain the difficulty in overcoming such a vigorous enemy defence, and stated that too much had been asked of his men, but Simonds would have none of it. With Simonds considering relieving the Polish brigadier and disbanding his command, only the intervention of two senior Canadian officers – Lt-Gen Crerar and Lt-Gen Kenneth Stuart, Chief of Staff, Canadian First Army – dissuaded him. The commander of Canadian 4th Armoured Division, Maj-Gen George Kitching, similarly questioned his superior's plans that emphasized having armour lead an attack along very narrow, 1km-wide frontages, but to no avail. Several days later Simonds sacked Kitching, and continued to imply that the Poles were responsible for the failure of Operation *Totalize*.

ANALYSIS

CROMWELL

During 7th Armoured Division's landing on D+1 (7 June 1944) the Cromwell's moderate size and weight proved well-suited for seaborne transport using the specially designed LCTs (Landing Craft, Tanks) and LSTs (Landing Ship, Tanks). In concert with a low tide, save for a few Cromwells that sank in unexpectedly deep water, the great majority of vehicles were able to advance directly inland and remove their waterproofing. When the British advanced towards Villers-Bocage on 10 June, 4th CLY and 5th RTR personnel encountered increasingly stiff German resistance while moving through very restrictive terrain that did not accord with their training or expectations, and employing combined-arms doctrine better suited to open environments. Through tactical adaptation and closer coordination with available infantry, as well as artillery, the Cromwells provided the requisite battlefield impact during the early coastal fighting expected of them.

Two months later the much more open country between Caen and Falaise presented the Cromwells of Polish 1st Armoured Division with an opportunity to showcase their strengths in spearheading rapid, deep-penetration armoured thrusts. The goal of Operation *Totalize*, however, was comparatively limited – to draw German armour away from interfering with the American break-out in the west. Instead of overwhelming already stretched German resources the resulting narrow Allied frontage presented potentially vulnerable flanks and a limited area in which 10th Mounted Rifle Regiment's Cromwells could operate, and produced a rather crowded battle zone that concentrated and constrained Allied freedom of movement and limited the use of available armour within the space provided. Heavy Allied aerial bombing and

A 5th RTR Cromwell Mk Vw passes infantry south of Caumont, France on 1 August 1944. A formation sign identified the parent brigade, division or corps, with 7th Armoured Division using its famous red jerboa in a white circle within a red square, while 22nd Armoured Brigade sported a red stag head. A coloured Arm of Service square with a unit serial number superimposed upon it identified the regiment, with 1st RTR, 5th RTR and 4th CLY having a red square with '51', '52' and '53' respectively in white to designate seniority. Geometric symbols denoted a tank's squadron, with Cromwells of an armoured reconnaissance regiment being white, while those in armoured brigades used red, yellow or blue in descending order of seniority. A, B, C and HQ squadrons used triangles, squares, circles and diamonds, respectively, and if displayed, troop numbers were placed within the squadron marking. A white star was often placed on the turret roof or rear for aerial identification, friend or foe. (The Tank Museum 3579-D4)

artillery shelling was intended to disrupt and eliminate German defences and facilitate Allied movement southwards, but the severely cratered roads, destroyed bridges and devastated urban areas ultimately hindered Allied movement and momentum.

Although the Cromwell weighed 4 tonnes more than the Jagdpanzer IV, its reliable Rolls-Royce Meteor engine produced nearly 600bhp (447kW) and 21bhp/tonne (15.7kW/tonne) – roughly double those of its opponent – which imparted excellent speed and mobility, but the very restricted *bocage* terrain in which it fought largely negated these assets. Although the Cromwell was at a considerable disadvantage against German Panthers and infrequent Tigers, and received mixed reviews from its crews, it was not intended to fight enemy tanks head-on, but rather leave such tasks to the supporting Sherman Fireflies or Challengers. Considering the much greater numbers of PzKpfw IVs, and equivalent designs, the Cromwell's armour and firepower offered parity, but the British vehicle was best suited to exploitation and pursuit roles. Despite the Cromwell's assets, which would prove to be a definite benefit during the largely fluid fighting in September 1944 and between February 1945 and the war's end, it remained under-gunned compared to its Firefly and Comet contemporaries. Like its domestically produced peers, the Cromwell's relatively light weight facilitated maintenance, and unlike the heavy German Tiger I and II largely negated the need to have bridges reinforced for crossing.

The Cromwell represented a markedly improved tank compared to its Covenanter and Crusader predecessors, but its crews expressed mixed feelings about the design, with many desiring to continue using their US-built Shermans. Because the 6-pdr's breech recoil hindered loading during operation, crews often removed its protective guard and canvas bag in spite of the safety risk. Although the Cromwell possessed similarities with the ubiquitous Sherman, the British tank's 6-pdr cannon lacked sufficient high-explosive capabilities and its flat armour reduced the vehicle's effectiveness in deflecting flat-trajectory projectiles compared to sloped equivalents. The Cromwell represented a considerable achievement for British industry, but the rapid pace of improved armoured-vehicle designs and capabilities, ammunition, and high manufacturing output meant that the design was arguably one to two years behind the newest German equivalents, and was often unfairly blamed for failures that

were more often deficiencies in supply, command and tactics. Ultimately, the Cromwell was best employed in open territory where its speed, manoeuvrability and reliability were assets in wide-ranging mobile operations and not a stand-up attritional fight.

JAGDPANZER IV

During the Normandy fighting the Jagdpanzer IV's low profile allowed it to excel when operating from obscured positions and ambushing unsuspecting enemy armour, before repositioning to another similar hull-down location to repeat the engagement pattern. With the Panzer-Lehr-Division having arrived piecemeal in the area around Tilly-sur-Seulles the formation made good use of what were essentially defensive assets during the effort to counter 7th Armoured Division and force it to redirect its thrust southwards. The Jagdpanzer IV's low centre of gravity proved beneficial in ascending and descending uneven ground, but its L/48 main gun's overhang was a hindrance for the unwary driver negotiating the confined *bocage* country, with its many woods and covering foliage, and could overstress the vehicle's transmission. With the main gun just 1.4m above the ground many crews removed the muzzle brake due to the considerable dust it could throw up when firing, thereby exposing the vehicle's position or obscuring effective targeting. Within the confined terrain around Tilly-sur-Seulles the Jagdpanzer IV represented a strong, mobile defensive asset within a formation doctrinally intended for offensive operations.

During Operation *Totalize* the Jagdpanzer IV crews, like other German armour units, operated much as they had done in June 1944: under the threat of Allied ground-attack aircraft that limited daytime movement and necessitated the use of the region's woods and copses for cover. As no vehicle successfully functions in a vacuum,

Because periscopes and vision slits limited visibility from inside an armoured vehicle, tank commanders routinely exposed themselves during combat operations to better spot the direction of sudden enemy fire, select targets, and coordinate with other troop vehicles. With British crews refraining from wearing helmets so as to not interfere with their headsets, sniper fire and shrapnel took a toll on commanders, especially in close terrain that enabled enemy infantry to get close to their mounts. This Cromwell IV from 2nd Northamptonshire Yeomanry (11th Armoured Division) is passing through the largely deserted town of Vassy on 15 August 1944. With the Falaise Pocket nearly closed the formation fought along its western edge near Flers, while some 50km to the east 12. SS-Panzer-Division *Hitlerjugend* continued to fight Polish 1st Armoured Division, which attempted to close the remaining German escape corridor near Chambois. With the Luftwaffe largely absent during the Normandy campaign the foliage would help break up the vehicle's profile and blend it into the surrounding terrain during ground operations. The readily accessible cables were used for towing disabled tanks. (The Tank Museum 1802-B3)

In August 1944 the Jagdpanzer IV began transitioning from its 7.5cm PaK 39 L/48 cannon to the more powerful 7.5cm PaK 42 L/70 cannon – the latter being the same weapon as found on the Panther, but with a different mounting. With two primary manufacturers 930 Jagdpanzer IV/70(V) (Vogtländische Maschinenfabrik AG) and 278 Jagdpanzer IV/70(A) (Altmärkische Kettenwerk GmbH) variants were produced by the war's end. Significantly longer than the L/48, the L/70's considerable overhang meant it needed to be held in a barrel lock during movement to avoid damage to its mechanical components and misalignment of its sighting equipment. Drivers also needed to be vigilant to avoid the barrel striking the ground or obstacles when moving over rough or constricted terrain. While the L/48 was built atop a modified PzKpfw IV Ausf H and was designated to carry 79 rounds, the L/70(V) and (A) were mated to newer PzKpfw IV Ausf H and Ausf J models respectively; these held longer, but fewer projectiles. The Jagdpanzer IV/70(V) shown here in an ambush camouflage scheme on 20 December 1944 is serving with SS-Panzerjäger-Abteilung 12 during the Ardennes Offensive. (Photo by US Army/The LIFE Images Collection/Getty Images)

the integration of available combat-engineer, artillery and *Panzergrenadier* formations led by officers experienced in creating ad hoc battlegroups at lower tactical unit levels helped promote SS-Panzerjäger-Abteilung 12's battlefield success, however small its relative contribution. Facing a more concentrated number of Allied armoured vehicles, however, SS-Panzerjäger-Abteilung 12 was able to inflict a disproportionate amount of damage from obscured, semi-static positions, while conducting an active defence. While the terrain during Operation *Totalize* was considerably more open, woods and farmland still permitted the low-profile Jagdpanzer IV to operate from concealed positions, as part of a fighting withdrawal.

As opposed to ad hoc anti-tank solutions, such as the Marder, the Jagdpanzer IV was the first Heereswaffenamt AFV designed specifically as a tank destroyer. Greatly increased production of the reliable PzKpfw IV in 1944 meant that its chassis was available in sufficient numbers to provide the foundation for several variants. It also had the benefit of being familiar to crews and mechanics, and not requiring major manufacturing and logistical changes. Both the 7.5cm PaK 39 L/48 and StuK 42 L/70 (in the form of the Panther's KwK 42) were already in production and would serve, along with its variants, as the primary German tank and anti-tank gun during the war. The PzKpfw IV's armour protection was considered adequate for 1943/44, and with metallurgical improvements unlikely to be introduced, the Jagdpanzer IV's sloped plate provided roughly twice the equivalent thickness as the turreted version, without incurring a weight increase. While tanks remained in production until the war's end, vehicles concurrently built atop their chassis, such as the Jagdpanzer IV, represented a cost-effective solution to maintain quality, increase quantity, and provide a counter to the much greater volume of enemy armour being produced and fielded. Within these configurations the Jagdpanzer IV represented a strong, mobile defensive asset within a formation doctrinally intended for offensive operations.

AFTERMATH

British forces disembarking at Gold Beach were caught largely by surprise at having to fight in the very constricted terrain that covered much of the Normandy battlefield, but individual formations in the field steadily developed successful solutions to overcome doctrinal and organizational constraints and limitations. While the Cromwell possessed similar characteristics and capabilities to those of the American Sherman, which saw a wide variety of variants and modifications, such as the Firefly, the British design represented more of a move towards what would be Montgomery's desired capital tank that embodied characteristics of the infantry and cruiser types. In early June 1944, the British sought to effect a rapid penetration of an initially porous German defence by using tactics that stressed armour–infantry coordination over integration at the 'minor tactics' level, with infantry employing the vulnerable Universal Carrier transports. This meant the Cromwell often fought with minimal immediate infantry support, save for when clearing built-up areas or protecting night-time laager positions. As Britain could ill-afford to fight an attritional, casualty-inducing war, caution and a desire for well-planned operations translated into delays, such as the build-up to organize 7th Armoured and 50th Infantry divisions around Bayeux between 7 and 9 June 1944. The Panzer-Lehr-Division, rapidly entering the battle zone, was able to slow the British assault at a time when speed and decisive action were warranted. While Panzerjäger-Lehr-Abteilung 130 provided a comparatively small combat element, its Jagdpanzer IV crews employed their mounts at critical battlefield sectors to contribute to German tactical successes. With the British halted before the road hub of Tilly-sur-Seulles the invaders pushed further west to an area that remained sparsely defended and from which a renewed effort to secure Villers-Bocage and the nearby high terrain would be made.

Although the Germans were forced to allocate formations piecemeal to contest the Allied effort to expand their bridgeheads, insufficient British reconnaissance around

Polish Cromwell IVs from 10th Mounted Rifle Regiment pass through Caen, which fell on 20 July 1944. Under the auspices of blocking German reinforcements from entering Second (British) Army's sector, Allied heavy bombers successively levelled most of the ancient city over five weeks for little appreciable effect, save destroying infrastructure and causing hundreds of non-combatant casualties, and the lingering resentment of many Norman citizens. (AFP/Getty Images)

22nd Armoured Brigade's narrow tactical thrust and the fortuitous position of schwere SS-Panzer-Abteilung 101 conspired to surprise and nearly destroy 4th CLY, which had recently halted having reached Villers-Bocage. The Cromwells stood little chance against the Tiger I's high-velocity 8.8cm cannon and very thick frontal armour, and although the aggressive, arguably reckless attack that was characteristic of Waffen-SS personnel was soon halted, 7th Armoured Division's forward elements prudently pulled back to their start line. Although the Cromwells would have proven an asset in what was expected to be a deep-ranging assault designed to unhinge German defences west of Caen, the solidifying front line forced the British and Canadians to conduct several offensives over the next six weeks to achieve a successful operational penetration to break into the relatively open terrain south and east of Falaise.

With Operation *Totalize* having had a promising beginning for Anglo-Canadian forces, high casualties among their two armoured divisions and an unexpectedly tenacious German defence intent on holding the 'Falaise Gap' open as long as possible prompted the offensive's cancellation on 13 August 1944. While Second (British) Army continued southwards out of Caen, the Americans overran most of Brittany before turning their full focus towards reaching the River Seine and helping seal off the roughly 150,000 Germans to prevent them from escaping eastwards. Immediately after the conclusion of Operation *Totalize*, Canadian and Polish forces began their final offensive in Normandy. Intent on capturing the town of Falaise, and then Trun and Chambois, around which Second (British) Army would progressively eliminate German escape routes and logistics support, Polish 1st Armoured Division and First (Canadian) Army commenced Operation *Tractable* immediately after Operation *Totalize*.

This photo shows one of the few Challengers produced. Much as the makeshift solution of incorporating a high-velocity 17-pdr cannon into an American M4 – the Sherman VC Firefly – had proven an effective anti-tank option, a similar effort transformed the British Cromwell into the Challenger (A30). As the Cromwell's turret lacked sufficient internal space to accept such a lengthy weapon and provide a stable platform on which it could effectively operate, a new turret was developed, which required an increase in ring diameter from 1,524mm to 1,778mm. This necessitated the upper hull extend over the tracks, and to compensate for a lengthened hull and to minimize ground pressure a sixth road wheel was added. To accommodate the required elevation angles the turret height was increased, which resulted in a higher vehicle profile than that of the original Cromwell. Although the Firefly lacked the speed to maintain a battlefield tempo alongside the faster Cromwell and 75mm Sherman, it was much easier to produce than the Challenger, and ultimately ten times as many were manufactured. While Challenger crews enjoyed its relatively roomy turret and a main armament that could effectively engage heavier German armour at reciprocal ranges, the design was rather unnecessary, as more purpose-built tanks, such as the Comet, with its slightly less effective 77mm HV (high-velocity) main gun, were being fielded. (The Tank Museum 10561-001)

A slow start allowed an increasingly desperate and fragmented German defence to mount delaying resistance effectively, but Crerar managed steady, but limited gains. By 19 August Maczek had partially closed the pocket during his drive on Chambois. Although the 'Falaise Gap' was narrowed to just a few kilometres, heavy fighting between battlegroups of Polish 1st Armoured Division and 12. SS-Panzer-Division *Hitlerjugend* resulted in thousands of German soldiers escaping eastwards to fight another day. With vehicles becoming trapped and destroyed in the congestion along an ever-dwindling number of extraction routes, German forces streamed eastwards, predominantly on foot. During two days of nearly continuous fighting, Polish artillery barrages and close-quarter fighting succeeded in holding off counter-attacks from seven trapped German divisions. On 21 August, elements of First (Canadian) Army relieved the Polish survivors and sealed the 'Falaise Pocket' by linking up with Third (US) Army, and forced the exhausted and trapped remnants of 7. Armee to surrender.

With the Westheer lacking the strength, support or will to establish any kind of stand along the River Seine the Germans quickly withdrew towards the relative safety of the German border. With speed a critical factor in pursuing and destroying a demoralized enemy and recapturing France and the Low Countries, the Cromwell finally found a chance to excel. 1st RTR and 5th RTR continued to operate under 22nd Armoured Brigade until the war's end, while what remained of 4th CLY merged with 3rd CLY on 1 August. During 7th Armoured Division's advance to the German border and the fighting into 1945 their Cromwells continued to provide acceptable service when employed in suitably mobile operations. Unlike the 'Desert Rats', who continued to outfit their armoured regiments with the Cromwell, the Polish 10th Mounted Rifle Regiment employed them in more accepted roles as armoured reconnaissance. While Polish forces fought with tenacity and a desire to avenge their nation's defeat in 1939, the war's end would prove bittersweet. With the British, Americans and Soviets having agreed to post-war European spheres of influence, many Polish soldiers from 1st Armoured Division felt Churchill and Roosevelt had betrayed them as they were prevented from continuing the fight by liberating their country from the occupying Soviets, who quickly established a brutal, authoritarian rule for the next four decades.

BIBLIOGRAPHY

PRIMARY

Bayerlein, Fritz. *Die PLD vom D-Tag bis zum V-Tag*, manuscript.
Brasche, Rudolf. *Kampfberichte der 1./901*, manuscript.
Ernst, R. *Panzerschlacht von Tilly*, manuscript.
Job, Eduard. *Kampfberichte der 3./Pz.Jäg.Lehr-Abt. 130*, manuscript.
Thies, Ernst. *Sie kommen*, manuscript.

SECONDARY

Buckley, John (2004). *British Armour in the Normandy Campaign*. Abingdon: Routledge.
Cloudsley-Thompson, John (2006). *Sharpshooter*. London: Arcturus Press.
Jacquet, Stéphane (2010). *Tilly-sur-Seulles: 7–26 June 1944*. Bayeux: Heimdal.
Jones, Keith (1990). *64 Days of a Normandy Summer: With a Tank Unit After D-Day*. London: Robert Hale.
Kucia, Przemysław (2011). *10th Mounted Rifle Regiment (1921–1944)*. Lubecka: Adam Marszałek.
Meyer, Hubert (1994). *The 12th SS: The History of the Hitler Youth Panzer Division Volume* I. Winnipeg: J.J. Fedorowicz.
Ogorkiewicz, Richard M. (1991). *Technology of Tanks*. Coulsdon: Jane's Information Group.
Perrigault, Jean-Claude (1995). *La Panzer-Lehr-Division*. Bayeux: Heimdal.
Place, Timothy Harrison, Dr. (2000). *Military Training in the British Army, 1940– 1944: From Dunkirk to D-Day*. Abingdon: Routledge.
Ritgen, Helmut (1979). *Die Geschichte der Panzer-Lehr-Division im Westen: 1944– 1945*. Stuttgart: Motorbuch-Verlag.
Spayd, P.A. & Wilkins, Gary, eds (2007). *Bayerlein: After Action Reports of the Panzer Lehr Division Commander from D-Day to the Ruhr*. Atglen, PA: Schiffer.
Számvéber, Norbert (2012). *Waffen-SS Armour in Normandy: The Combat History of SS Panzer Regiment 12 and SS Panzerjäger Abteilung 12, Normandy 1944*. Solihull: Helion.
Wasilewski, Jerzy (1947). *10 Pułk Strzelców Konnych w kampanii 1944–45* (*10th Mounted Rifle Regiment Campaign, 1944–45*). Nuremberg: self-published.
Wilson, Edward (2003). *Press on Regardless: The Story of the Fifth Royal Tank Regiment in World War Two*. Staplehurst: Spellmount.
Wysocki, Tadeusz A. (1994). *1. Polska Dywizja Pancerna, 1939–1947: geneza i dzieje* (*1st Polish Armoured Division, 1939–1947: Origin and history*). Warsaw: Bellona.

OTHER

British Intelligence Objectives Sub-committee (1946). 'German Tank Armour'.

British War Office (1943a). 'The Co-operation of Infantry and Tanks'. Army Training Instruction No. 2 (May 1943).

British War Office (1943b). 'The Tactical Employment of Armoured Car and Reconnaissance Regiments'. Military Training Pamphlet No. 60.

British War Office (1944). 'Tank Fire Tactics'. MTP No. 34. Royal Armoured Corps Weapon Training, Part 4 (April 1944).

Combined Intelligence Objectives Sub-Committee. 'Interrogation of Herr Stiele[r] von Heydekampf'. Evaluation Report No. 153, 28 June 1945.

Holborn, Andrew (2009). 'The role of 56th (Independent) Infantry Brigade during the Normandy campaign June–September 1944'. Thesis.

NAC, RG 24, Vol. 10942, File 245.P1.013(D1), 'Operational Report, C.O. 1st Polish Armoured Division Fighting During the Period from 7–12 Aug 1944', 13 August 1944.

RG 24 Vol. 10.554 Appx 'J', to 21 Army Group RAC Liaison Letter No. 5, 'Extract from Report by Medical Research Section on the Distribution of Casualties Amongst the Crews of Cromwell and Sherman Tanks', 28 August 1945, 2.

Telephone Log, Kriegstagebuch des Panzer-Armeeoberkommando 5 10.6.44– 8.8.44. RH19 IX/M.

Vojenský historický archiv, Praha (Military History Archives, Prague), Anlagen zum KTB der SS-Panzer-Jager-Abteilung 12 'Hitlerjugend', Gefechbericht fur 9.8.1944/1. (schw.)/SS-Pz.Jag.Abt. 12 'HJ'.

Watertown Arsenal Laboratory (1945). 'Metallurgical Examination of British Homogeneous and Face Hardened Armor'.

Williams, Ethan, LCDR (2007). '50 Div in Normandy: A critical analysis of the British 50th (Northumbrian) Division on D-Day and in the battle of Normandy'. Thesis.

WO 171/456. 11th Armoured Division, War Diary. The National Archives, UK.

WO 171/619. 22nd Armoured Brigade, War Diary. The National Archives, UK.

WO 171/856. 4th County of London Yeomanry, War Diary. The National Archives, UK.

WO 171/865. 1st Royal Tank Regiment, War Diary. The National Archives, UK.

WO 171/867. 5th Royal Tank Regiment, War Diary. The National Archives, UK.

WO 208/3647. Interrogation of SS-Sturmbannführer Jacob Hanreich. The National Archives, UK.

INDEX